EZRA POUND

EZRA
POUND
The Image and the Real

Herbert N. Schneidau

LOUISIANA STATE UNIVERSITY PRESS BATON ROUGE

Copyright © 1969 by
LOUISIANA STATE UNIVERSITY PRESS

Library of Congress Catalog Card Number: 75–86495

SBN 8071-0911-8

Manufactured in the United States of America by Thos. J. Moran's Sons, Inc.

Designed by Robert L. Nance

To Barbie

PREFACE

This book is about Ezra Pound's poetics, with some observations on the theory of knowledge in the background of most of his poetry. For my purposes, the subject is best treated in the context of two of the major efforts of Pound's life: one was the Imagist Movement itself, and the other was his constant striving to reach what J. Hillis Miller has perceptively called "the poetry of reality." Within both of these efforts inhered a reverence for the precisely presented particular, which Pound sometimes called the "Luminous Detail"; this reverence shaped a theory of knowledge so broad as to include without tension a strain of rationalism (as seen in Pound's respect for Santayana's philosophy or Agassiz' scientific method) and a pronounced interest in mysticism, especially some of its medieval varieties. This ability to resolve traditional antitheses of thought is symptomatic, and corresponds to a basic principle of his poetics, which unified a traditional dichotomy between the creative energy of the artist and the structure or form of his art-work: rejecting the assumption that form must contain or mold force, Pound insisted that force must create form and be defined only through it. Both resolutions of antitheses depend on that reverence for "Luminous Detail." Ultimately this reverence implies a faith, a confidence in the close and illuminating relation of *visibilia* to *invisibilia*— or, to use terms I employ later, the particular to the universal. For Pound this was a faith in reality itself: instructed by some of his mystical friends, he believed that the true poet "interprets" a universe full of mysteries but nonetheless in every sense *real*. Perhaps the word "magus" is the core of the word "Imagism" after all.

My speculations on these subjects are presented by means of discussing the impact that some of Pound's friends had on his poetics, and the study assumes some knowledge of the basic facts of Pound's career e.g., that he left America for London in 1908, that in 1912–14 he publicized Imagism through Harriet Monroe's fledgling *Poetry* magazine, and that Amy Lowell took the movement away from him in 1914, creating what he called "Amygism." In conclusion I advance some suggestions about simple and obvious yet relatively unexplored ways to study Pound's work more deeply.

I would like to thank most gratefully the following persons for various kinds of help and encouragement, though without implying responsibility for any of my errors or wrongheaded views: Carlos Baker, Joseph N. Riddel, Roy Harvey Pearce, and Hugh Kenner.

H.N.S.

CONTENTS

EZRA POUND

ONE

IMAGISM AS DISCIPLINE
Hueffer and the Prose Tradition

IT IS NOTHING NEW to say that the basis of Ezra Pound's poetics may be seen in the Imagist Movement that Pound himself brought to being in 1912 in London. Yet Imagism remains a somewhat cloudy business. Despite all the work that has been done on it, one might say that the movement itself has been studied with less clarity and brilliance than have its relations with post-Symbolist aesthetics. Many discussions of Imagism content themselves with superficial repetitions, and Pound's most gifted interpreter, Hugh Kenner, has been reduced to saying that the history of Imagism is "a red herring." [1] This is not true, though it is a laudable attempt to clear Amy Lowell and other large obstacles out of the way of Pound criticism, but I would agree that no "theory of the Image" currently talked about helps much to illumine Pound's poems. The repetitions about Imagist theory have obscured the fact that the earliest focus of Imagism was on a discipline involving what Pound called "living language" and "presentation," not on any theories of the Image as such. Slightly later the focus shifted to include more theoretical concerns, but the discipline remained the heart of the

[1] Hugh Kenner, *The Poetry of Ezra Pound* (London, 1951), 58.

achievement, yielding poems that employed severe artistic control to make a few words carry a large burden of meaning. This discipline was derived to a significant degree from ideas and attitudes of Pound's good friend, the novelist Ford Madox Hueffer (later Ford Madox Ford). When talking about Hueffer's relation to them, Pound spoke of these ideas as "the prose tradition."

Pound's pre-Imagist poetry lacked this discipline, and his early poetics was a *mélange* of Aestheticism, scientistic "realism," and Browningesque "vigor" that Pound later mocked as "red-blooded." He described the first two elements in a letter written to William Carlos Williams in 1908: pre-eminent among his poetic aims, he wrote, were "beauty" and "freedom from didacticism" combined with a diagnostic objectivity: "I record symptoms as I see 'em. I advise no remedy. I don't even draw the disease usually. Temperature 102 ⅜, pulse 78, tongue coated, etc., eyes yellow, etc." [2] The third element, Browningesque vigor, shows in most of the poems of this period that are not over-suffused with the pale glow of Aestheticism. Two stanzas from "Cino" are typical:

> 'Pollo Phoibee, old tin pan, you
> Glory to Zeus' aegis-day,
> Shield o' steel-blue, th' heaven o'er us
> Hath for boss thy lustre gay!

> 'Pollo Phoibee, to our way-fare
> Make thy laugh our wander-lied;
> Bid thy 'fulgence bear away care.
> Cloud and rain-tears pass they fleet!

Even as burlesque it is rather painful. That last line especially

---

[2] *Letters of Ezra Pound, 1907–1941*, ed. D. D. Paige (New York, 1950), 4–6. Hereinafter cited as *Letters*.

must have made Pound squirm when he formed a mature style. That this vigor represents Pound's idea of Browning is evident in the poem "Mesmerism," in which friendly mockery of "ye old mesmerizer's" style is mixed with the dregs of an adolescent enthusiasm for it:

> You wheeze as a head-cold long-tonsilled Calliope,
> But God! what a sight you ha' got o' our in'ards,
> Mad as a hatter but surely no Myope,
> Broad as all ocean and leanin' man-kin'ards.

The "first fine careless rapture" that engendered those rhymes, and the sense of humor that let them stand, paid for their liveliness by producing effects that in the end seem more grotesque than vigorous. Some of the juvenilia reach surprising heights in spite of their affectations, even for a taste as squeamish as mine: while I find "Sestina: Altaforte" a thundering bore, I confess to admiring "Ballad of the Goodly Fere," which has less sentimentality than one might expect, and has a dramatic force in the last lines not unlike certain effects in Yeats's early poetry: "I ha' seen him eat o' the honey-comb/ Sin' they nailed him to the tree." What Pound was trying to do in these lines can perhaps be glossed by a comment he made years later on Shakespeare's *Pericles:*

> *Faith, she would serve, (pause)*
> *after a long voyage at sea.*

The cadence is so well-taken that even the archaism in the first word doesn't dim the naturalness of the sentence.[3]

There are fine things in the earlier poems, but there is about them a sense of strain, of trying too hard to make a book of

3 *Ibid.*, 299.

"Poems." Some, like "Portrait d'une Femme," are clear forecasts
of the mature style, but the poeticisms, inversions, archaisms,
and other remnants of "using it [Provence] as subject matter,
trying to do as R. B. had with Renaissance Italy," weigh heavily
on most.[4]

The first step of Imagism was to jettison this excess baggage.
Pound had decided by December, 1911, that a new mode was
necessary for himself, and for the health of English poetry. In
an essay significantly entitled "Prolegomena," he wrote:

As to Twentieth century poetry, and the poetry which I expect
to see written during the next decade or so, it will, I think, move
against poppy-cock, it will be harder and saner, it will be what
Mr. Hewlett calls "nearer the bone." It will be as much like granite as it can be, its force will lie in its truth, its interpretative
power (of course, poetic force does always rest there); I mean it
will not try to seem forcible by rhetorical din, and luxurious
riot. We will have fewer painted adjectives impeding the shock
and stroke of it. At least for myself, I want it so, austere, direct,
free from emotional slither.[5]

This is more an exaggerated repudiation of embarrassing juvenilia than an accurate prescription for a new mode, but the passage has the true Puritanic tang of Imagism. The vocabulary used
underlines the severities of the discipline Pound thought necessary: note the strong moralistic tone resulting from terms like
"luxurious riot," "painted adjectives," and "poppy-cock." The
desirable mode, on the other hand, is characterized in rigid un-

---

[4] *Ibid.*, 179. Pound put the matter fairly bluntly when he said "it takes
six or eight years to get educated in one's art, and another ten to get rid of
that education. . . . I hadn't in 1910 made a language, I don't mean a language to use, but even a language to think in." See *Literary Essays of Ezra
Pound*, ed. T. S. Eliot (Norfolk, Conn., 1954), 194. Hereinafter cited as
Literary Essays.

[5] The essay was first published in *Poetry Review*, I (1912), 72–76; it is
more conveniently found in *Literary Essays*, with the quotation on p. 12.
A footnote on p. 12 dates the passage December, 1911.

compromising words: it would be "like granite," strike the reader with its "shock and stroke," stand out from mere effusions by being "austere, direct, free from emotional slither."

The tone of the passage from "Prolegomena" suggests that words like "direct" in the original Imagist concordat have more hortatory, disciplinarian flavor than Pound's description indicates:

In the spring or early summer of 1912, "H. D.," Richard Aldington and myself decided that we were agreed upon the three principles following:
1.   Direct treatment of the 'thing' whether subjective or objective.
2.   To use absolutely no word that does not contribute to the presentation.
3.   As regarding rhythm: to compose in the sequence of the musical phrase, not in sequence of a metronome.[6]

The first two points stress control and excision; the third point does too, since in reality it was an attack on the flabby practice of filling up rhythmic spaces with empty words. Pound used a similarly disciplinarian vocabulary in the letter urging Harriet Monroe to introduce "Imagisme" to the world in the form of H. D.'s poems: "I've had luck again, and am sending you some *modern* stuff by an American, I say modern, for it is in the laconic speech of the Imagistes, even if the subject is classic. . . . Objective—no slither; direct—no excessive use of adjectives, no metaphors that won't permit examination. It's straight talk, straight as the Greek!" [7]

Pound's next gift to Miss Monroe was his own series, "Contemporania"; it was not granitic, indeed he termed it "ultra-modern, ultra-effete tenuity," but it fulfilled most of the other

[6] "A Retrospect," first published in Pound's *Pavannes and Divisions* (New York, 1918); see *Literary Essays*, 3.
[7] *Letters*, 11.

expectations for the new mode, and clearly represents the first-
fruits of Imagist discipline in his own work. The title itself emphasizes Pound's sense of emerging from antiquarianism, and
the abrupt change of style is often the subject of these pieces:

> O my fellow sufferers, songs of my youth,
> A lot of asses praise you because you are "virile,"
> We, you, I! We are "Red Bloods"!
>
>   ("The Condolence")
>
> You were praised, my books,
>   because I had just come from the country;
> I was twenty years behind the times
>   so you found an audience ready.
> I do not disown you,
>   do not you disown your progeny.

> Here they stand without quaint devices,
> Here they are with nothing archaic about them.
> Observe the irritation in general . . .
>
>   ("Salutation the Second")

The "Contemporania" poems indicate that Imagism was first of
all an ascetic means of dissolving impurities and of resolving the
poem into "straight talk," a classic directness in the accents of
contemporary speech. Next they imply a new freedom of attitude, a new unpretentiousness of subject, a new brilliance in the
use of himself as *persona*—all taking rise from Pound's desire to
bid good-bye to his earlier style, and the postures in which it had
involved him. Finally, although these poems neither rely on visual images nor conform very well to any "theory of the Image"
as usually understood, we must face the fact that no visualization requirement nor theory of the Image is listed among the
points agreed upon by Pound, H. D., and Aldington, nor recorded by Aldington in his reminiscences of the movement.

What theory there would be was only groping toward articulation in Pound's mind at that early stage, and what he strove to impress on his young friends was a new discipline. The well-known "A Few Don'ts," Pound's first pronouncement of Imagist doctrines to the public, had originally been designed as a rejection slip for *Poetry* magazine.[8]

As "Prolegomena" tells us, one of the targets of this new movement was something in nineteenth-century poetry called "rhetorical din." Pound shared this aversion to rhetoric with many artists of his time, but his remedy for it is exceptional and revealing. Whereas for many of his contemporaries the "nondiscursive *concetto*" transplanted from the age of the Metaphysicals to newer, post-Symbolist soil was the efficacious charm against rhetoric, Pound recommended that the poet achieve classic directness by studying neither seventeenth-century nor Symbolist poetry but nineteenth-century prose: "Poetry must be *as well written as prose.* Its language must be a fine language, departing in no way from speech save by a heightened intensity (i.e. simplicity). There must be no book words, no periphrases, no inversions. It must be as simple as De Maupassant's best prose, and as hard as Stendhal's." [9] The "Contemporania" series, as full of prosaicisms as the earlier poems had been of poeticisms, shows Pound groping toward a more natural diction and rhythm by using the prose antidote.

In the same letter to Harriet Monroe from which the above passage is taken (written in 1915, after the full fruition of Imagism), Pound spelled out what a poetics derived from prose might aim at:

[8] *Ibid.,* 78–79. For Aldington's reminiscences, see his autobiography, *Life for Life's Sake: A Book of Reminiscences* (New York, 1941), esp. pp. 133–37. Also see his letter reproduced in *Ezra Pound: Perspectives,* ed. Noel Stock (Chicago, 1965), 122–24.

[9] *Letters,* 48–49. In 1918 Pound again recommended "the actual language, i.e., all that has made my stuff interesting since 'Contemporania' " (*Letters,* 127).

There must be no clichés, set phrases, stereotyped journalese. The only escape from such is by precision, a result of concentrated attention to what [he] is writing. The test of a writer is his ability for such concentration AND for his power to stay concentrated till he gets to the end of his poem, whether it is two lines or two hundred.

Objectivity and again objectivity, and expression: no hindside-before-ness, no straddled adjectives (as "addled mosses dank"), no Tennysonianness of speech; nothing—nothing that you couldn't, in some circumstance, in the stress of some emotion, actually say.

Here we see a usable definition of "precision," combined with an extreme insistence on real language, proposed as the cure for rhetoric and like diseases. In expanding on his reasons for this belief Pound wrote: "When one really feels and thinks, one stammers with simple speech; it is only in the flurry, the shallow frothy excitement of writing, or the inebriety of a metre, that one falls into the easy—oh, how easy!—speech of books and poems that one has read." This confession suggests again that Imagism involved a conversion from an imitative style, but still more significant is a footnote later attached to this passage that names the counselor of the conversion: "It should be realized that Ford Madox Ford had been hammering this point of view into me from the time I first met him (1908 or 1909)." [10] What Pound specifically had in mind when he recommended prose as a discipline, and what he meant by saying that "the 'Imagisme' of 1912 to '14 set out 'to bring poetry up to the level of prose,' " can best be understood by examining Pound's relations with Hueffer, the friend of James and collaborator with Conrad.[11]

[10] The footnote was first printed in Harriet Monroe's autobiography, *A Poet's Life: Seventy Years in a Changing World* (New York, 1938), but may be found in *Letters*, p. 49.

[11] Pound's statement is from "Vorticism," which first appeared in the *Fortnightly Review*, XCVI (1914), 461–71, reprinted in Pound's *Gaudier-Brzeska: A Memoir*. In the edition that I used (New York, 1961), the quotation is on p. 83.

"Mr. Hueffer has preached 'Prose' in this Island ever since I can remember," wrote Pound in reviewing Hueffer's *Collected Poems* in 1913. " 'Prose' is his own importation. There is no one else with whom one can discuss it. . . . Because of his long prose training Mr. Hueffer has brought into English verse certain qualities which younger writers would do well to consider." [12] Pound very much wanted the younger writers, especially his Imagists, to consider these qualities; as he put it in "A Few Don'ts": "Don't think any intelligent person is going to be deceived when you try to shirk all the difficulties of the unspeakably difficult art of good prose by chopping your composition into line lengths. . . . Don't imagine that a thing will 'go' in verse just because it's too dull to go in prose." [13] If indeed a certain mastery of the art of prose was almost a prerequisite for good verse, who was better fitted to instruct in this art than one of the most dedicated novelists of the day? Pound's shepherding of his young friends was largely responsible for turning the villa South Lodge, where Hueffer held forth, into a "stamping ground for *les jeunes*." [14] There Hueffer the fabulist told endless stories peopled with the great literary figures he had known; there Pound, who had moved from earlier lodgings near the British Museum to Kensington, fairly close to South Lodge, picked up a rich fund of anecdotes—many of the stories in a book of Hueffer's like *The Critical Attitude* (1911) later turn up in Pound's writings.[15] "I made my life in London by going to see

[12] "Ford Madox Hueffer," *New Freewoman,* I (1913), 251.

[13] "A Few Don'ts by an Imagiste" was first published in *Poetry,* I (1913), 200–206; see *Literary Essays,* 5–6.

[14] Douglas Goldring, *South Lodge: Reminiscences of Violet Hunt, Ford Madox Ford and the English Review Circle* (London, 1943), 47.

[15] For instance, Hueffer wrote this: "Nothing was more true than the words of Flaubert, when he said that, if France had read his 'Education Sentimentale' she would have been spared the horrors of the Franco-Prussian War." Pound wrote in his essay on James: "Flaubert said of the War of 1870: 'If they had read my *Education Sentimentale,* this sort of

Ford in the afternoons and Yeats in the evenings," Pound recalled many years later.[16]

At first, however, Pound seems to have valued Hueffer's conversation only for the anecdotes, not for the doctrines about
writing; in fact, he resisted Hueffer's literary ideas for several
years. After acting as Hueffer's secretary for some weeks in 1911,
Pound wrote to his mother that he disagreed with Hueffer "diametrically" on every question: "art, religion, politics." [17] It is
not hard to discover where the basic quarrel was. Hueffer scoffed
that "most of the verse that is written today deals in a derivative
manner with medieval emotions," a remark possibly aimed at
Pound directly, and set himself uncompromisingly against the
kind of poetic diction that Pound allowed himself in the early
poems.[18] Hueffer's own principle, in spite of his connections
with Pre-Raphaelite and Victorian figures, was to use only the
contemporary language:

I may really say that, for a quarter of a century, I have kept before me one unflinching aim—to register my own times in terms
of my own time, and still more to urge those who are better
poets and better prose-writers than myself to have the same aim.
. . . It is somewhat a matter of diction. In France, upon the whole,
a poet—and even a quite literary poet—can write in a language

thing wouldn't have happened.' " (Cf. Ford Madox Hueffer, *The Critical
Attitude* [London, 1911], 29, with *Literary Essays,* 297.) Again, Hueffer
reports that "Mr. James came to Europe and studied Turgenev. Mr.
Howells remained in America and studied Mr. Henry James" (p. 93).
Pound's version: "American literature from 1870 to 1910 is summed up in
the sentence: 'Henry James stayed in Paris reading Flaubert and Turgenev.
Mr. William Dean Howells returned to America and read the writings of
Henry James.' " See his letter in *Little Review,* IV (1917), 38.

[16] Donald Hall, "Ezra Pound: An Interview," *Paris Review,* 28
(Summer-Fall, 1962), 36.

[17] From a letter in the American Literature Collection of the Yale University Library which Mr. Donald Gallup kindly let me see.

[18] Hueffer, *The Critical Attitude,* 187.

that, roughly speaking, any hatter can use. In Germany, the poet writes exactly as he speaks.[19]

In his Imagist phase Pound propagandized for a real language of the times more forcefully than Hueffer ever did, but it is interesting to note that only a few months before the creation of the movement, he had been fighting a dogged rear-guard action against this very principle; he wrote that "colloquial poetry is to the real art as the barber's wax dummy is to sculpture," and "there are few fallacies more common than the opinion that poetry should mimic the daily speech." [20] Even in an article not published until March, 1912, Pound continued to resist, but his arguments were weakening: "Mr. Hueffer is so obsessed with the idea that the language of poetry should not be a dead language, that he forgets it must be the speech of to-day, dignified, more intense, more dynamic, than to-day's speech as spoken." [21]

Pound's balkiness on this point is worth more investigation, for not only was he concerned to defend his own pre-Imagist practice, but also seems to have thought that his other master, Yeats, counterbalanced Hueffer's weight as an authority. In an interview in 1962 Pound stated, "I went to London because I thought Yeats knew more about poetry than anybody else. . . . I went to study with Yeats and found that Ford disagreed with him." He further pointed out that Ford deserves some of the credit usually given to Pound himself for the hardened style of

[19] From an essay printed in *Poetry*, II (1913), 177–87, as "Impressionism— Some Speculations." A note in *Collected Poems by Ford Madox Ford* (New York, 1936), 323, says the essay was actually written in 1911. It can be found most conveniently in *Critical Writings of Ford Madox Ford*, ed. Frank MacShane (Lincoln, Neb., 1964), quotation on p. 141. Hereinafter cited as *Critical Writings*.

[20] "En breu brisaral temps brau," *New Age*, X (1912), 370.

[21] Review of Hueffer's *High Germany*, in *Poetry Review*, I (1912), 133. This appeared in March, but was no doubt written somewhat earlier.

the "later Yeats": "As far as the change in Yeats goes, I think that Ford Madox Ford might have some credit. Yeats never would have taken advice from Ford, but I think that Fordie helped him, via me, in trying to get towards a natural way of writing." [22] But this process took time, for especially in those days Yeats was for Pound a "great dim figure with its associations set in the past"; as I have argued elsewhere, his aim in studying with Yeats was not to learn about the future of poetry but its past, and Yeats presented him with no demand to discontinue the use of archaistic and derivative devices.[23] In fact Pound seems to have valued Yeats as a kind of medium who could bring him into communication with the dead, just as his only interest in Hueffer at first was in the fund of anecdotes about the great dead. Writing of Lionel Johnson, a ghost he knew through Yeats, Pound approved Johnson's "curial" diction, and his rearguard action against Hueffer employed the same term: "We must have a simplicity and directness of utterance, which is different from the simplicity and directness of daily speech, which is more 'curial,' more dignified." [24] By 1915, however, Hueffer had long since made his point, and Pound reversed himself: "Now Lionel Johnson cannot be shown to be in accord with our present doctrines and ambitions. His language is a bookish dialect, or rather it is not a dialect, it is a curial speech and our aim is natural speech, the language as spoken." [25]

Besides Yeats, a group of influential literary figures befriended by Pound in his first years in London seems to have buttressed his resistance to Hueffer's arguments. Later Pound regretted being swayed by this group, who formed an "arthritic milieu

---

[22] Hall, "Ezra Pound: An Interview," 36, 30.

[23] Pound's description of Yeats is from *Letters*, 21; my argument is in "Pound and Yeats: The Question of Symbolism," *ELH*, XXXII (1965), 220–37.

[24] "En breu brisaral temps brau," 370.

[25] Preface to the *Poetical Works of Lionel Johnson* (London, 1915); see *Literary Essays*, 362.

that held control of the respected British critical circles, New-bolt, the backwash of Lionel Johnson, Fred Manning, the Quar-terlies and the rest of 'em." [26] In retrospect, Pound nominated Hueffer's brief tenure as editor of the *English Review* (1908–1909) as the first breakaway from this arthritic milieu toward literary modernism: "The man who did the *work* for English writing was Ford Madox Hueffer (now Ford). The old crusted lice and advocates of corpse language knew that *The English Review* existed." But at the time, he added sorrowfully, he hadn't known what Hueffer was really doing. "Don't think that I read *The Eng. Rev.* then. . . . Nothing to be proud of, but so was it. I was learning how Yeats did it." [27] And, he might have added, he was very friendly with those "old crusted lice." Sir Henry Newbolt, Frederic Manning, and G. W. Prothero (editor of the *Quarterly Review*) were treated with great deference in Pound's early letters and writings.

At that time, as later, Pound thought Yeats a mystic-minded Symbolist as well as a voice out of the past. "Learning how Yeats did it" therefore involved some toying with Symbolist practices, such as the use of what J. Hillis Miller calls "indefinite, suggestive, emotive images . . . of the right blurred sort," or what Pound called "vague suggestion" which enabled a poet to deal with "the ineffable." [28] In *The Spirit of Romance* (1910) Pound used Yeats as the type of "atmospheric suggestion," con-trasted to Dante's precision; in 1913 he made it clear that Hueffer stood in direct opposition to this Symbolist tradition:

I would rather talk about poetry with Ford Madox Hueffer than with any man in London. Mr. Hueffer's beliefs about the

[26] From Pound's obituary of Hueffer in *Nineteenth Century and After*, CXXVI (1939), 180.

[27] *Letters*, 296.

[28] J. Hillis Miller, *Poets of Reality: Six Twentieth-Century Writers* (Cambridge, Mass., 1965), 150; Pound, "On Technique," *New Age*, X (1912), 298.

art may be best explained by saying that they are in diametric opposition to those of Mr. Yeats. Mr. Yeats has been subjective; believes in the glamour and associations which hang near the words. 'Works of art beget works of art.' He has much in common with the French symbolists. Mr. Hueffer believes in an exact rendering of things. He would strip words of all 'association' for the sake of getting a precise meaning.[29]

This passage yields three important reasons why Hueffer's ideas finally won out. First, Pound could never really bring himself to respect Symbolism as a movement: as he said in 1914, "One does not want to be called a symbolist, because symbolism has usually been associated with mushy technique." [30] Second, the phrase "works of art beget works of art" suggests that Pound identified Yeats with the derivative style, the trap of falling into the "speech of books and poems that one has read." Hueffer longed to free writing from this habit: "What worried and exasperated us in the poems of the late [Victorians] . . . is their imitative handling of matter, of words; it is their derivative attitude"; he lamented that "the poets of today record their emotions at receiving the experience of the emotions of former writers." [31] Finally, Pound admired the principle of stripping words of association to get a precise meaning—a problem brought to his attention, Hueffer said, by Conrad.

Conrad's indictment of the English language was this, that no English word is a word: that all English words are instruments for exciting blurred emotions. 'Oaken' in French means 'made of oak wood'—nothing more. 'Oaken' in English connotes innumerable moral attributes: it will connote stolidity, resolution, honesty, blond features, relative unbreakableness, absolute unbend-

---

[29] *The Spirit of Romance* (Norfolk, Conn., 1953), 159; "Status Rerum," *Poetry*, I (1913), 125.

[30] *Gaudier-Brzeska,* 84–85. (From the "Vorticism" essay of 1914; see note 11.)

[31] *Critical Writings,* 151.

ableness—also, made of oak. . . . The consequence is, that no English word has clean edges.[32]

For all these reasons Pound stopped trying to forge a poetics from Yeatsian ideas, and sought the "hard-edged" quality that Hueffer's doctrines seemed to promise. Curiously enough, his personal friendship with Yeats became even stronger after aesthetic discipleship was out of the question.

The methods Hueffer used to win this debate were somewhat sarcastic, but effective because they were applied directly to Pound's problems. He rolled on the floor laughing and groaning at the archaisms in one of Pound's early volumes of verse, for instance.[33] In an essay written apparently in 1911 for his own *Collected Poems* (later sent by Pound to Harriet Monroe as "the best prose we've had or are likely to get"), Hueffer qualified slightly his sneer at verse that dealt "in a derivative manner with medieval emotions" by admitting that he found "suggestions of power in Mr. Pound's derivations from the Romance writers," but he insisted also that "Mr. Pound, as often as not, is so unacquainted with English idioms as to be nearly unintelligible." In the same essay, Hueffer conceded a value to historicism, not mentioning Pound by name but choosing examples that reflect some of Pound's interests:

This is not saying that one should not soak oneself with the Greek traditions; study every fragment of Sappho; delve ages long in the works of Bertran de Born; translate for years like the minnelieder of Walther von der Vogelweide; or that we should forget the bardic chants of Patric of the Seven Kingdoms. . . . Let us do anything in the world that will widen our perceptions. We are the heirs of all the ages. But, in the end, I feel fairly assured that the purpose of all these pleasant travails is the right

[32] *Ibid.*, 88.
[33] Pound's obituary of Hueffer, *Nineteenth Century and After*, 179; cf. Hall, "Ezra Pound: An Interview," 30.

appreciation of such facets of our own day as God will let us perceive.[34]

Hueffer insisted on the unchanging nature of experience: unless he has the courage to look at and portray life, the modern poet will "never realize that Paolo and Francesca loved and suffered precisely as love and suffer the inhabitants of the flat above him." [35] This kind of statement did more than make Pound a modernist; it gave him the clue for a new non-derivative way to use his scholarly research into the past, and the idea of an unchanging basis of experience is certainly a key to his later poetry, especially the *Cantos*.

Pound may have been grateful that Hueffer saw the use of lore from the past, but by the time of Imagism he had become committed to modernism in any case. In fact the very word "modern" in his writings of this period is usually a sign that Hueffer's ideas were present. His comment on Hueffer in the "Prolegomena" of December, 1911, was cool and reserved but still prophetic: "Ford Hueffer is making some sort of experiments in modernity"; a remark he made in 1913 about D. H. Lawrence, one of *les jeunes* sponsored by Hueffer, provides another example: "Detestable person but needs watching. I think he learned the proper treatment of modern subjects before I did. That was in some poems in *The Eng. Rev.*" [36] Reviewing Lawrence's poems, Pound praised only those in the "daily speech" of coal-country dialect, and related them to the prose tradition: "His prose training stands him in good stead in these poems. . . . Mr. Lawrence has attempted realism and attained it. He has brought contemporary verse up to the level of contem-

---

[34] *Critical Writings*, 149, 152, 145. (See note 19 concerning the 1911 date.)
[35] *The Critical Attitude*, 187.
[36] *Letters*, 17.

porary prose, and that is no mean achievement." [37] "To bring poetry up to the level of prose" was precisely the goal that Pound set for Imagism; his awarding this palm to a man he detested is best explained not only by his disinterestedness but also by his evident belief that prose disciplines were the common source of Lawrence's and Imagism's attainment of "living language."

It may be hard for us to understand why Hueffer had such trouble awakening Pound to the peculiar vitality and authority of an oral basis for poetry. Today we are so acutely aware of the potencies of the language as spoken that one often discerns in our art the assumption that if we could capture "the way people really talk" we could hold reality in our hands. In our time the precise use of real language has a supreme value; Twain's achievement in manipulating five dialects in *Huckleberry Finn* is really a modern discovery, remarkable mostly by our standards: one can imagine a nineteenth-century critic struggling to comprehend the relevance of this feat to the art of the novel. Now, even secondary disciplines like foreign-language study and dictionary-making produce their monuments, the "language lab" and *Webster's Third*, to the acceptance of the spoken language as primary, normative, and life-giving. The "oral basis" has become an orthodoxy; it is like Coleridge's theory of the imagination, of which I. A. Richards remarks that today "a doctrine of the creative mind [is] so familiar that we may even wonder how men have ever failed to hit on [it]." [38] To be sure, a call for the real language of men is at least as old as Wordsworth, but the nineteenth-century heritage faced by the poets of the early twentieth century included very few responses to this call. Even Wordsworth failed to grasp its real meaning;

[37] Review of *Love Poems and Others*, *Poetry*, II (1913), 150–51; cf. *Literary Essays*, 388.

[38] I. A. Richards, *Coleridge on Imagination*, Midland ed. (Bloomington, 1960), 16.

many critics, beginning with Coleridge, have pointed out that
his best work does not exemplify the principle. The nineteenth
century was impeded by an overvaluation of the *permanence* of
written language, well dramatized by Thoreau:

There is a memorable interval between the spoken and the written language, the language heard and the language read. The one
is commonly transitory, a sound, a tongue, a dialect merely, almost brutish, and we learn it unconsciously, like the brutes, of
our mothers. The other is the maturity and experience of that;
if that is our mother tongue, this is our father tongue, a reserved
and select expression, too significant to be heard by the ear,
which we must be born again in order to speak.

  .   .   .   .

A written word is the choicest of relics.[39]

In the age of the "happening" we rather equate permanence
with death, but in those days transience vs. permanence was a
one-sided debate. The similarity of Pound's earlier ideas about
"curial" diction to some of Thoreau's phrasing indicates the
weight of the heritage he had to cast off. At any rate, Hueffer
impressed Pound with the need to use the language as spoken
with a precision unknown to Wordsworth, drawn from the
"prose tradition": "Since March 1913, Ford Madox Hueffer has
pointed out that Wordsworth was so intent on the ordinary or
plain word that he never thought of hunting for *le mot juste*."
So, although the young Imagist was urged to read "as much
of Wordsworth as does not seem too unutterably dull," Pound
looked to the prose tradition as the true source.[40] The new precision in the use of language tells in the work: Pound developed
a subtler ear for speech-cadences than any nineteenth-century
poet. When Charles Olson proclaims that "speech is the 'solid'

[39] Henry David Thoreau, "Reading," *Walden*.
[40] *Literary Essays*, 7; cf. 373, and *Gaudier-Brzeska*, 115: "The common
word is not the same thing as the *mot juste*, not by a long way."

of verse, is the secret of a poem's energy," he dates the discovery back to Pound's work and the "revolution of the ear, 1910." [41] Only in our century have Olson and others been able to see the whole problem of separation between the poet's voice and the printed page.

For all the immense significance of the principle of living language, Imagism itself was at least as dependent on another principle that Pound seems to have adapted from Hueffer's ideas. Like the mastery of real speech, this was a method that involved acquiring and practicing a severe discipline. The essence of the method was concealed, for Pound, within the innocuous-looking word "presentation." We have seen the word already, in such Imagist formulae as "directness of presentation," and "no word that does not contribute to the presentation," but its most important appearance is in the well-known definition of the Image articulated by Pound in 1913:

An 'Image' is that which presents an intellectual and emotional complex in an instant of time. I use the term 'complex' rather in the technical sense employed by the newer psychologists, such as Hart, though we might not agree absolutely in our application.
It is the presentation of such a 'complex' instantaneously which gives that sense of sudden liberation; that sense of freedom from time limits and space limits; that sense of sudden growth, which we experience in the presence of the greatest works of art.[42]

Understandably distracted by the portentous-looking "complex," critics have failed to notice that Pound was using "presentation" to mean something more than "handing over." Yet Pound goes on in "A Few Don'ts," where the definition is found, to make it very clear that he is employing a technical term:

[41] Charles Olson, "Projective Verse," in *The New American Poetry: 1945–1960*, ed. Donald M. Allen (New York, 1960), 391, 386.
[42] *Literary Essays*, 4.

"When Shakespeare talks of the 'Dawn in russet mantle clad'
[*sic*] he presents something which the painter does not present.
There is in this line of his nothing that one can call description;
he presents." Close attention to this passage should suffice to get
rid of the notion that Imagism implied a "viewy" kind of poetry
analogous to representational art. It may have fallen into mere
pictorialism later, but that was under Amy Lowell's hegemony.
Once again the idea of visualization can be misleading: it was
not "pictures in verse" that Pound wanted, but something with
the hard-edged quality, the sharp definition, that the visual
sense furnishes. Pound's friend May Sinclair, evidently aware of
Pound's distinction, wrote of Imagism that "Presentation not
Representation is the watchword of the school." [43] This was in
effect another way of stating Pound's determination to present
rather than describe experience.

Another injunction from "A Few Don'ts" that uses the term
is a capsule form of Pound's version of literary history: "Consider the definiteness of Dante's presentation, as compared with
Milton's rhetoric." When he expanded this into a full survey of
world literature in *How to Read* (1929), Pound stressed the
virtue of maintaining definiteness and avoiding rhetoric in literature:

The individual cannot think and communicate his thought, the
governor and legislator cannot act effectively or frame his laws,
without words, and the solidity and validity of these words is in
the care of the damned and despised *litterati*. When their work
goes rotten . . . i.e. becomes slushy and inexact, or excessive or
bloated, the whole machinery of social and of individual thought
and order goes to pot.

.   .   .   .

It is not only a question of rhetoric, of loose expression, but also
of the loose use of individual words. What the renaissance gained
in direct examination of natural phenomena, it in part lost in

[43] "Two Notes," *Egoist*, II (1915), 88.

losing the feel and desire for exact descriptive terms. I mean that the medieval mind had little but words to deal with, and it was more careful in its definitions and verbiage.[44]

Here and in other places in the essay Pound suggested that a definiteness of presentation like that of Dante and a precise terminology go hand in hand. He also used the example of two poets who achieved exact presentation by reacting against "imperial and sentimental exploitations" in the language of their times: "In Rimbaud the image stands clean, unencumbered by nonfunctioning words; to get anything like this directness of presentation one must go back to Catullus, perhaps to the poem which contains *dentes habet*." In Pound's judgment, Catullus and Rimbaud thus exemplify the first and second of the three Imagist points. In between these two, according to Pound, an age of decorated language came in with the fading of medieval "exactness": "After Villon, and having begun before his time, we find this *fioritura*, and for centuries we find little else. Even in Marlowe and Shakespeare there is this embroidery of language, this talk about the matter, rather than presentation." The result was that poetry eventually lost its title as a vehicle of clear presentation, and Stendhal realized that prose could replace poetry as such a vehicle: "And at that moment the serious art of writing 'went over to prose,' and for some time the important developments of language as means of expression were the developments of prose. And a man cannot clearly understand or justly judge the value of verse, modern verse, any verse, unless he has grasped this." Indeed Pound believed that good modern poetry depended absolutely on the developments of the nineteenth-century French novel: "I believe no man can now write really good verse unless he knows Stendhal and Flaubert. . . . To put it perhaps more strongly, he will learn more about the art

[44] First printed in *New York Herald Tribune Books* in January, 1929; see *Literary Essays*, 21–22.

of charging words from Flaubert than he will from the floribund sixteenth-century dramatists." [45]

Pound regarded "presentation" as the important part of the legacy from Stendhal and Flaubert. Writing to René Taupin about the ancestry of Imagism, Pound disavowed Symbolist influence, and summarized his own work aside from metrics in two phases: "Ma *reforme:* 1. Browning—denué des paroles superflus 2. Flaubert—mot juste, présentation ou constatation." [46] Later he linked the second part of this *"reforme"* directly to Hueffer:

The revolution of the word began so far as it affected the men who were of my age in London in 1908, with the LONE whimper of Ford Madox Hueffer. . . . Hueffer (Ford) read Flaubert and Maupassant in a way that George Moore did not. Impressionism meant for him something it did not to Mr. Symons.

.   .   .   .

Mr. Hueffer was getting himself despised and rejected by preaching the simple gallic doctrine of living language and *le mot juste.*[47]

"Le mot juste," as we see from the letter to Taupin, was for Pound equivalent to "présentation" or "constatation." Writing about the technique of a French poet, Laurent Tailhade, who had had the benefit of being nourished on Stendhal and Flaubert, Pound invented the term "prose tradition" to embody these values:

I think this sort of clear presentation is of the noblest traditions

---

[45] *Literary Essays,* 33, 29, 31, 32.

[46] *Letters,* 218.

[47] *Polite Essays* (London, 1937), 50, 10; cf. *Gaudier-Brzeska,* 115, which reprinted an essay of 1915 on the contributions of various people to the decade: "Ford Hueffer, a sense of the *mot juste.* The belief that poetry should be at least as well written as prose, and that 'good prose is just your conversation.' This is out of Flaubert and Turgenev and Stendhal, and what you will. It is not invention, but focus."

of our craft. It is surely the scourge of fools. It is what may be called the "prose tradition" of poetry, and by this I mean that it is a practice of speech common to good prose and to good verse alike. . . . It means constatation of fact. It presents. It does not comment. It is irrefutable because it does not present a personal predilection for any particular fraction of the truth. . . . The presentative method is equity. It is powerless to make the noble seem ignoble. It fights for a sane valuation.[48]

The lessons of Flaubert against "comment" are familiar enough now. It only remains to add that for Pound "comment" and "rhetoric" were more or less identical enemies, and that Hueffer was the mediator of the "prose tradition" or "presentative method" that opposed these. In an article for *Poetry* in 1914 called "Mr. Hueffer and the Prose Tradition In Verse," Pound praised Hueffer's practice and principles: "It is he who has insisted, in the face of a still Victorian press, upon the importance of good writing as opposed to the opalescent word, the rhetorical tradition." Pound ended the essay by remarking, "I find him significant and revolutionary because of his insistence upon clarity and precision, upon the prose tradition; in brief, upon efficient writing—even in verse." [49] If clarity and precision were concomitants of the presentative method, its ultimate aim was "efficiency"—making every word count. In "The Serious Artist" (1913), full of praise for a kind of scientific accuracy in art, Pound tried to define the supreme value in poetry thus: "On closer analysis I find that I mean something like 'maximum efficiency of expression'; I mean that the writer has expressed something interesting in such a way that one cannot re-say it

[48] "The Approach to Paris," *New Age*, XIII (1913), 662.
[49] *Poetry*, IV (1914), 111–20; *Literary Essays*, 371–77. I find that Kenner, Noel Stock, and I have used these same quotations in almost the same way. This is not, I hope, due to unconscious plagiarism, but to the utility of the phrases. Stock, in *Poet in Exile: Ezra Pound* (New York, 1964), treats the Hueffer-Pound relationship very ably, as does Kenner, but both neglect some of the Imagist connections.

more effectively." [50] Perhaps that definition is a clue to what happened to convince him finally of the justice of Hueffer's arguments; once in trying to take notes on a scene in a Hueffer novel, Pound said, "[I] found to my surprise that I couldn't make the note in fewer words than those on Ford's actual page." [51]

Hueffer's own uses of the words "presentation" and "constatation" leave little doubt as to how Pound came to use them. In *The Critical Attitude*, Hueffer visualized the truly modern artist: "He too will *constater*, not colour, the life of which he treats." [52] He used the word "presentation" in the same honorific way: "You attempt to involve the reader amongst the personages of the story or in the atmosphere of the poem. You do this by presentation and by presentation and again by presentation." [53] The difference between a novel by "the forgotten James Payne" and the "unforgettable author of *The Turn of the Screw*," he wrote, "is that the one recounts whilst the other presents." [54] He used the term again to explain Conrad's successful technique:

There is one technical maxim that jumps at the eye all through his work. It is this: *Never state: present.* And again: *Never state: present.* . . . And yet this does not really exhaust the matter—for, of course, statements must be used; indeed, paradoxically, the author of this school has nothing to use but statements. And perhaps a more exact statement of the maxim (for the words *"Never state: present!"* are a sort of slang of technical phraseology), perhaps an exact lay rendering of the maxim would be *"Never comment: state."* [55]

[50] First published in the *New Freewoman*, I (1913); see *Literary Essays*, 56.
[51] Pound's obituary of Hueffer, *Nineteenth Century and After*, 180.
[52] *The Critical Attitude*, 35.
[53] *Critical Writings*, 43; the essay was first published in 1913.
[54] *Ibid.*, 59.
[55] "Joseph Conrad," *English Review*, X (1911), 76–77.

In support of these maxims Hueffer offered the explanation that "the author must make the events narrated strike the senses as nearly as possible as they would be presented by nature herself." The aim of "presentation," or "statement" in this sense, is the veridical registration of the form of an experience. This aim dominates Imagist poetry: each poem seeks to register an experience, an emotion, or a state of mind with what might now be called "presentational immediacy."

So far the discipline was largely negativistic; the emphasis was on precision, concision, and excision. But the ultimate goal was positive; if an author refrained from comment, his work had to be the more exact, especially when the presentation was to communicate "intellectual and emotional complexes." A definition of Imagist presentation by Richard Aldington illuminates the technique: "We convey an emotion by presenting the object and circumstance of that emotion without comment. For example, we do not say 'O how I admire that exquisite, that beautiful, that—25 more adjectives—woman' . . . but we present that woman, we make an 'Image' of her, we make the scene convey the emotion." [56] The most important point made here is that "Image" refers not to the usual literary device of that name but to a set of lasting impressions, a configuration that one "gets" of something or someone. We have already seen that the Imagists did not have in mind the standard meaning of "representation," and they also were not thinking of the literary usages signifying "vague picture" or "vivid metaphor." They meant something far more comprehensive, something capable of presenting whole complexes of ideas, something like "a manifestation of essence" or "an epiphany." The Imagist "Image" is Hueffer's "impression" raised several powers. There need be nothing esoteric in such broader conceptions of the term: we have a more worldly version of the Imagist meaning whenever a businessman talks

[56] "Modern Poetry and the Imagists," *Egoist*, I (1914), 202.

about his company's image, or a politician about his own. Without a more comprehensive definition Pound would have been unable to make statements like "Dante's 'Paradiso' is the most wonderful *image*." [57] Certainly it is a mistake to think of "imagery" as an equivalent: May Sinclair said that "imagery is one of the old worn-out decorations the Imagists have scrapped." [58]

Perhaps the best illustration of the intended method is contained in an anecdote that Pound probably gleaned from Hueffer's talk: "It is said that Flaubert taught De Maupassant to write. When De Maupassant returned from a walk Flaubert would ask him to describe someone, say a concierge whom they would both pass in their next walk, and to describe the person so that Flaubert would recognize, say, the concierge and not mistake her for some other concierge and not the one De Maupassant had described." When retailing this for the benefit of his young protégée Iris Barry, Pound commented: "That is the way to write poetry." [59] To achieve Flaubert's object an attempt must be made to "present a complex instantaneously," to delineate the concierge in a few essential details that will make her uniqueness leap out at the reader; in the terms of art history, a perceptual image must be stripped down to the essences that constitute a conceptual image. Those critics who have discerned a connection between this doctrine and Joyce's "epiphanies" seem to me on the right track; the aim is an exactness of registration that will manifest the uniqueness of the object or situation, that Scotistic *haecceitas* which Joyce called *quidditas* (mistakenly) after Aquinas.

The similarity of Images to "epiphanies" of realities implies that the method aims at nothing less than a kind of secular revelation. If Pound had not thought of Imagism with some such

57 *Gaudier-Brzeska*, 86.
58 "Two Notes," 88.
59 *ABC of Reading* (New York, 1960), 65; originally published in 1934. See also *Letters*, 92.

end in mind he could hardly have said that "it is better to present one Image in a lifetime than to produce voluminous works." [60] To be sure, there are those who say that such talk is merely backwash from Symbolism, and Imagism has often enough been written off as merely a "local version" of Symbolist aesthetic.[61] Without attempting to deny the necessarily post-Symbolist character of all these epiphanic concepts, I would contend that such claims are somewhat misleading. First, there is in Imagism very little of the typical Symbolist aspiration toward nondiscursive ineffability: Pound turned away from that, in effect, when he dropped the attempt to adopt a Yeatsian-mystic aesthetic. Second, Imagism tries to "convey an emotion by presenting the object and circumstance of that emotion without comment"; would it not be more typically Symbolist strategy to try to present the emotion without the object—to present whatever thought and feeling are caused by an event, but to withdraw any mention of the event? I suspect Pound formulated his own critique of this aspect of Symbolism when he wrote that "the proper and perfect symbol is the natural object." Some of Pound's poems are similar to Symbolist "enigmas without keys" (such as "The Return," which Yeats liked), but they are the exceptions.[62]

My separation of Imagism from Symbolism can be tested by a look at a poem that seems to embody Imagism as discipline very well, better even than such well-known set-pieces as "In a Station of the Metró." I refer to "The Garden," first published in the "Contemporania" series, which presents an image of a woman not by multiplying adjectives but by making the scene convey the emotion:

[60] *Literary Essays*, 4.
[61] Specifically by Frank Kermode, in *Wallace Stevens* (New York, 1961), 11.
[62] Pound's remark was made in "Prolegomena"; see *Literary Essays*, 9, and cf. 5. For Yeats's preference, see *Poetry*, IV (1914), 27.

Like a skein of loose silk blown against a wall
She walks by the railing of a path in Kensington Gardens,
And she is dying piece-meal
            of a sort of emotional anemia.

And round about there is a rabble
Of the filthy, sturdy, unkillable infants of the very poor.
They shall inherit the earth.

In her is the end of breeding.
Her boredom is exquisite and excessive.
She would like someone to speak to her,
And is almost afraid that I
            will commit that indiscretion.

This is a post-Symbolist poem, and it profits by being so, but it hardly illustrates a local version of Symbolist aesthetic. On the other hand, Pound does seem to have aimed at a presentative "maximum efficiency of expression." How could the last lines possibly be more concentrated, unfolding as they do not only the agonizingly mixed motives of the woman but also the narrator's insight in which pity and contempt blend? Did not Pound in fact achieve the *mot juste* with "almost"? And does not the "end of breeding" exemplify poetic ambiguity in its best sense, with its interacting meanings of purpose, climax, degeneration, and *dernier cri?* There is even a homophonic suggestion of "inbreeding" which ties up all the rest, and places the emphasis on the bred-out sense. "Breeding" itself furnishes, in addition to disagreeable impressions of high-strung horses, just the right hint of bloodlines to bring back the earlier "anemia," which is itself linked to the mealy disintegration in "piece-meal." As for the other parts: the apparent redundancy of "filthy, sturdy, unkillable" is bitingly rectified by the double-edged ironies of "They shall inherit the earth"; the deceptively Ninetyish way in which the formal simile of the first line unfolds is seen to be concise and perfect for the image of the unraveling lady. Pound's celebrated mastery of rhythm also helps the sense of concentration: note how the cadence suggests an emphasis on the second syllable of "exquisite," so that a pretentious high-society note is made to ring also with overtones of nerves squeezed, wrung, drawn out too fine.

Notice that it is Pound the speaker, not Pound the author, who "comments," and that the thoughts are those of the moment of the experience, just enough "refined" to suit the theme perfectly. An essential part of Pound's presentation here is a degree of empathetic projection into the woman's world, and that involves a recognition of her idiom. She is not only rather afraid of her own thoughts, but she belongs to a class for which anything but extreme reserve in manners or speech is "bad form." Hence the poem uses much clipped understatement, contributing to the apprehension of the woman's state of mind and also to the sense of concentration upon which presentation depends. "No word that does not contribute to the presentation," "nothing you couldn't actually say"; these doctrines are points both for presentation *and* for living language, and for Pound the principles were interdependent. Of course it helps that in this case the living language does involve terse, restrained turns of phrase; an Image of a garrulous Texan or a voluble Italian might demand a language less congenial to the severities of presentation. These are not thereby precluded from Imagism: Pound solved a humorous problem along these lines in his poem "The Study in Aesthetics"; but the fact is that Imagism was best suited to post-Victorian London, and a few other situations in which reticence is the idiomatic norm. One of these other situations can be found in classical Chinese poetry, of which Pound made good use: in his poetic development, the phase of Imagism proper was followed by a period in which his main concerns were epigrams, *haiku,* and adaptations from Chinese. Here is one example of the latter, in which reticence and presentational condensation are carried to such a degree that Pound had to add a prose gloss:

The Jewel Stairs' Grievance
The jewelled steps are already quite white with dew,
It is so late that the dew soaks my gauze stockings,
And I let down the crystal curtain
And watch the moon through the clear autumn.

> Note.—Jewel stairs, therefore a palace. Grievance, therefore there is something to complain of. Gauze stockings, therefore a court lady, not a servant who complains. Clear autumn, therefore he has no excuse on account of weather. Also she has come early, for the dew has not merely whitened the stairs, but has soaked her stockings. The poem is especially prized because she utters no direct reproach.

The values of reticence for Imagist discipline could hardly be better illustrated, by the gloss as much as the poem—though the last sentence is a little explicit. At all events, why "the laconic speech of the Imagistes" should come to birth in London in 1912 should now be more understandable. We must remember that two of the three original Imagistes were young and impressionable Americans, and that the habitual understatement of the British educated classes must have seemed quite graceful to them: its influence can be seen in Pound's work even before Imagism.

One more point about Imagism may be abstracted from the fertile soil of "The Garden": the diagnostic impulse and disease-metaphor employed there were habitual with Pound, and have a correlation with his poetics; they go at least as far back as his stated intention to Williams to "record symptoms as I see 'em," and certainly are displayed in the definition of Imagism as presenting intellectual and emotional "complexes." We remember that Pound explicitly linked his notion of complexes to those of "the newer psychologists, such as Hart." Bernard Hart, M.D., was a pioneer in London psychiatry who described himself as under the influence of Freud, Jung, and Krafft-Ebing. Hart's meaning for "complex" appears to have been popularized in such phrases as "inferiority complex"; he defined them as systems of "emotionally toned ideas," operating unobserved in the mind, which caused random trains of thought to return continually to one object or feeling.[63] The Image, we remember, was to present such complexes instantaneously, as a photographer might try to capture in a chance gesture or unguarded expression some revelation of mood or personality traceable to a set of fixed ideas; but first the complex had to be diagnosed. A medical tone appears in much of Pound's poetry and prose—for instance, in the "Serious Artist," written at about the time of the creation of Imagism:

The arts give us a great percentage of the lasting and unassailable data regarding the nature of man, of immaterial man, of man considered as a thinking and sentient creature. They begin where the science of medicine leaves off or rather they overlap that science. The borders of the two arts overcross.

.   .   .   .

The cult of beauty is the hygiene, it is sun, air and the sea and the rain and the lake bathing. The cult of ugliness, Villon, Baudelaire, Corbière, Beardsley are diagnosis. Flaubert is diagnosis. Satire, if we are to ride this metaphor to staggers, satire is surgery, insertions and amputations.[64]

"Flaubert is diagnosis": to epiphanize a concierge he had to divine her particular complex. Perhaps the most revealing statement of this side of the matter is an observation made by Pound about the talents of a friend who profited from Imagism, Dr.

[63] See Bernard Hart, M.D., *The Psychology of Insanity* (Cambridge, 1912), Preface and Chap. Five.
[64] *Literary Essays*, 42, 45.

William Carlos Williams. Pound wondered "whether Williams himself isn't at his best—retaining interest in the uncommunicable or the hidden roots of the consciousness of people he meets, but confining his statement to presentation of their objective manifests." [65] The doctor must be skilled in diagnosing from a few visible signs—the kind that could be presented in an Image. There is after all a genuine affinity between medicine and certain kinds of literature in which observation is important: Conan Doyle, a doctor, modeled Sherlock Holmes on a medical school professor who had a knack for uncanny deductions from ordinary details. Perhaps Flaubert was only teaching De Maupassant techniques picked up from his family's medical background. In any case I believe that discussion of "presentation" can end with the observation that it consists of a mastery of proportion between detail and insight that would serve a diagnostician.

The question may arise here as well as anywhere: if so much credit is to be given to Hueffer for Imagism, exactly where did his contributions end and Pound's begin? Pound himself put the differentiation this way: "The Image is more than an idea. It is a vortex or cluster of fused ideas and is endowed with energy. If it does not fulfill these specifications, it is not what I mean by an Image. It may be a sketch, a vignette, a criticism, an epigram or anything else you like. It may be impressionism, it may even be very good prose." [66] For Pound, Hueffer was the good kind of Impressionist (as well as a master of "very good prose"): "Impressionism meant for him something it did not mean to Mr. Symons." Clearly he referred to Hueffer's technique when he said, "Imagisme is not Impressionism, though one borrows, or could borrow, much from the impressionist method of presentation." [67] In further characterizing the good kind of Impression-

[65] "Dr. Williams' Position," first published in the *Dial* in 1928; see *Literary Essays*, 398.
[66] "As for Imagisme," *New Age*, XVI (1915), 349.
[67] *Gaudier-Brzeska*, 85. (From the "Vorticism" essay of 1914.)

ist, as distinct from the "rosy, floribund bore" who writes "in imitation of Monet's softness," he put his finger on what Hueffer's work too often lacked. "There is," he said, "a school of prose writers, and of verse writers for that matter, whose forerunner was Stendhal and whose founder was Flaubert. The followers of Flaubert deal in exact presentation. They are often so intent on exact presentation that they neglect intensity, selection, and concentration. They are perhaps the most clarifying and they have been perhaps the most beneficial force in modern writing." [68] No doubt Pound thought that it would be the role of the "Image" to supply the desirable "intensity, selection, and concentration." That this should be the point of differentiation suggests that somewhere between 1912 and 1914 Pound discovered that Hueffer did not in fact often achieve "maximum efficiency of expression"; indeed, he seems to be talking about Hueffer again in the same essay: "An impressionist friend of mine talks to me a good deal about 'preparing effects,' and on that score he justifies much unnecessary detail." Probably this is what he meant when he remarked in 1962 that "Ford's stuff appeared too loose then, but he led the fight against tertiary archaisms." [69]

Yet even with the distinction in mind we can see that Pound retained his interest in prose disciplines for poetry long after Imagism proper was over; in fact, when he started composing longer poems he grew even more positive about the benefits to be derived. Thus he remarks in 1937 in admiring Hardy's *Collected Poems:* "Now *there* is a clarity. There *is* the harvest of having written 20 novels first." Still greater praise is this tribute: "Hardy is Gautier's successor as Swinburne cd. not be." [70] It has been quite hard for critics to understand Pound's reverence

[68] "Dubliners and Mr. James Joyce," first printed in *Egoist,* I (1914), 267; see *Literary Essays,* 399–400.

[69] *Literary Essays,* 401–402; Hall, "Ezra Pound: An Interview," 30.

[70] *Letters,* 294; *Guide to Kulchur* (Norfolk, Conn., 1952), 293.

for Hardy, "so much the last poet one would have expected Pound to admire" as Donald Davie wonderingly says. I suggest that the explanation can only be in the exaggerated reverence for prose which Hueffer first inculcated.[71] It was not affectation when Pound described *Mauberley* as "an attempt to condense the James novel," and "the definite attempt to get the novel cut down to the size of verse." [72] In a sense, many of his poetic ambitions are related to novelistic structures, especially if we disregard notions of plot and story, which Pound was all too ready to do. (He says for instance of Joyce's *Dubliners:* "He is not bound by the tiresome convention that any part of life, to be interesting, must be shaped into the conventional form of a 'story'. . . . Mr. Joyce's *Araby*, for instance, is much better than a 'story', it is a vivid waiting." [73]) Pound's longer poems have little use, we know, for plot, but they do have the interest in "sequences of consciousness" that marks a James novel. Even the obscure historical detail, puzzling allusion, and particularized reference in the *Cantos* might be considered roughly as Pound's improvement, as he would see it, upon a novelist's local detail. At least if we entertain this comparison we could grant Pound the same kind of indulgence we commonly grant to novelists, and stop trying to annotate everything.

There is a need for further investigation of the Hueffer–Pound relationship, which involved far more than a mere exchange of views; the pattern of Hueffer's life made him into a towering figure of the persecuted artist in Pound's mind. In those years his life was marred first by his failure to make the *English Review* pay, in spite of its brilliant contributors, and by divorce scandals and other improprieties. Pound brooded over the fact that Hueffer had been forced to sell the *Review* to Sir Alfred

---

71 Donald Davie, *Ezra Pound: Poet as Sculptor* (New York, 1964), 151.
72 *Letters*, 180; Hall, "Ezra Pound: An Interview," 33.
73 *Literary Essays*, 400.

Mond, and over Hueffer's ostracism (from a society which had never had much use for Pound himself). More and more Hueffer seemed to stand for "the serious artist," as Pound termed the real man of letters, and more and more evil seemed the motives of his persecutors. In 1914 Pound held up Hueffer as the lonely professional wearily defending his high standards against a genteel conspiracy of amateurs and dilettantes: "In a country in love with amateurs, in a country where the incompetent have such beautiful manners, and personalities so fragile and charming, that one cannot bear to injure their feelings by the introduction of competent criticism, it is well that one man should have a vision of perfection and that he should be sick to the death and disconsolate because he cannot attain it." [74] By 1937 the fragile amateurs, once Pound's good friends, had become "ole bastards," "old crusted lice and advocates of corpse language" who conspired against the man with the vision of perfection. Pound's conception of his own alienation from society is contained in that metamorphosis.

[74] *Ibid.*, 371.

TWO

HULME VS. FENOLLOSA

Image and Reality

HULME

IN READING over the accumulation of material on Imagism, one is struck by the perpetuation of certain myths. One such myth concerns the role in Imagism of T. E. Hulme. A suspicion exists that Pound literally stole Imagism from Hulme, given voice by Hulme's biographer Alun Jones, who says that Pound "took upon himself the credit of Hulme's Imagism." Mr. Jones somewhat weakens his case by admitting that Hulme's poems "do not belong to the Imagist movement as such," and that "his theory of poetry finds its most coherent expression neither in the poems of the Imagists, nor in his own poems, but in the early poetry of T. S. Eliot." [1] Still this claim has received a great deal of attention, so much that even those who have found little basis for the charge of theft feel compelled to make some kind of bow toward it. Thus Frank Kermode says that "Pound's own aesthetic is not fundamentally different from Hulme's, though he is quite right to insist that it was available to him without

[1] Alun R. Jones, *The Life and Opinions of T. E. Hulme* (Boston, 1960), 30, 53.

Hulme's mediation," and that "the principles of the Imagist manifesto . . . are all Hulmian." [2] Even the movement's chronicler, Stanley K. Coffman, Jr., "feels that Pound thought he was repeating Hulme" though he "borrowed only the most superficial aspects of Hulme's theory." [3] In spite of the lack of any convincing presentation of a case for theft, suspicions of Pound's honesty linger on, and are certainly not dispelled by such cautious judgments.

Yet what are the facts? An appraisal of Hulme's influence might begin with the note that the two contemporaries who propagated the idea of Hulme's primacy, F. S. Flint and John Gould Fletcher, make it clear that they begrudged Pound his success and greatly desired to discredit him. Fletcher seems to have felt that Pound had been trying to use him and his money.[4] Flint's authority in saying, after the "Amygist" revolt, that there was no difference between Imagist poems of 1915 and those produced by a circle that he and Hulme led in 1909, is open to further suspicion; even his fellow Amygist Aldington wrote at the time of the movement's origins: "We liked F. S. Flint, although the nearest he had got to Imagism was reading masses of young French poets and imitating Verlaine." [5] Aldington,

[2] Frank Kermode, *Romantic Image* (London, 1961), 121, 135.

[3] Stanley K. Coffman, Jr., *Imagism: A Chapter for the History of Modern Poetry* (Norman, Oklahoma, 1951), 181; also see Coffman's Ph.D. dissertation from which the book was adapted, "Imagism: The Contribution of T. E. Hulme and Ezra Pound to English Poetry, 1908–1917" (Ohio State University, 1948), 249. The latter contains some valuable material not in the book.

[4] *Life Is My Song: The Autobiography of John Gould Fletcher* (New York and Toronto, 1937), 62–63. See also Charles Norman, *Ezra Pound* (New York, 1960), 104, 110–11. Aldington indicates the unreliability of Fletcher's memory in *Life for Life's Sake* (New York, 1941), 133–34.

[5] F. S. Flint, "History of Imagism," *Egoist*, II (1915), 70–71. Wallace Martin, in *"The New Age" Under Orage: Chapters in English Cultural History* (New York and Manchester, 1967), says that Flint's statement "has usually been accepted as accurate; however, his hostility toward Pound at this time . . . may have coloured his account" (p. 153). Martin

who could never be accused of excessive love for Pound, viewed the matter as if the only possible theft could have been of the word "Imagisme" itself. "According to the record, Ezra swiped the word from the English philosopher, T. E. Hulme. . . . My own belief is that the name took Ezra's fancy, and that he kept it *in petto* for the right occasion." [6] I do not know what "record" Aldington was referring to, unless he meant what Flint had told him; if Flint's case against Pound convinced Aldington that only the name was involved, it cannot have been very substantial. It seems noteworthy that none of the Amygists showed any inclination to proclaim Hulme as leader when they had jettisoned Pound. As for Hulme himself, he never presented any claim that anyone but Fletcher remembered; he seems to have taken no interest in Imagism at all.

Pound's own words have been used against him, but only by being quoted in misleading contexts. It is true that he once told Glenn Hughes that Hulme "was an original or pre-" Imagist, but more often he tried to point out that ideas about Hulme's role had ballooned out of proportion: "Mr. Hulme is on the road to mythological glory; but the Hulme notes, printed after his death, had little or nothing to do with what went on in 1910, 1911, or 1912." [7] Such remarks proceeded from no grudge; Pound in all of his statements was extremely generous to Hulme. But he knew, of course, to whom any debt was owed: "Without malice toward T. E. H. it now seems advisable to correct a

---

also contributes this privileged observation: "[Pound's] letters to Flint . . . which have not yet been published, make it clear that Imagism as he conceived it had little to do with the discussions of the [Hulme-Flint group]" (p. 153). Flint was of course writing from an "Amygist" point of view, and may have been right that "Amygist" poems were not different from Hulme's. In any case he says that Edward Storer, not Hulme, led the discussions of the "Image" in the 1909 group. Aldington's comment is in *Life for Life's Sake*, 136.

[6] *Life for Life's Sake*, 135.

[7] *Letters*, 213; *Polite Essays*, 9.

distortion which can be found even in portly works of reference. The critical LIGHT during the years immediately pre-war in London shone not from Hulme but from Ford (Madox etc.) in so far as it fell on writing at all." [8] There is only one reference by Pound in the time of the movement to a connection between it and Hulme: the prose note attached to the "Complete Poetical Works of T. E. Hulme," printed by Pound as an appendage to his *Ripostes* in 1912. The five minuscule poems by Hulme had first been published, without any prose note, in the *New Age* in January, 1912, probably as a joke by Pound and *New Age* editor A. R. Orage. In the note in *Ripostes* Pound simply carries the joke further: he reprints them, he says, not as good poems but for "good fellowship" and because Hulme "sets an enviable example to many of his contemporaries who have had less to say" by finishing off a "Complete Poetical Works" at thirty.[9] This tone continues throughout the piece. Pound says that *Les Imagistes* are "descendants" of the "forgotten school of 1909," but calls that the " 'School of Images,' which may or may not have existed." Further, he muses that the discussions of this group were "dull enough at the time, but rather pleasant to look back on," and observes that their "principles were not so interesting as those of the 'inherent dynamists' or of Les Unanimistes, yet they were probably sounder than those of a certain French school that attempted to dispense with verbs altogether . . . ." The comparison with ephemeral Parisian groups was not especially flattering.

Two more bits of circumstantial evidence testify against the notion that Pound "thought he was repeating Hulme." Just be-

[8] "This Hulme Business," *Townsman*, II (1939), 15. Hugh Kenner reprinted the note in *The Poetry of Ezra Pound* (London, 1951), 307. See also *Letters*, 296.

[9] The note is most easily available in the volume that I have been using for citations of poems, *Personae: The Collected Shorter Poems of Ezra Pound* (New York, 1949), 251.

fore the creation of Imagism, we remember, Pound had written an essay called "Prolegomena," calling for a new mode in twentieth-century verse; he broad-mindedly named several writers who might be getting toward this mode from different directions, including Yeats, Robert Bridges, Maurice Hewlett, Frederic Manning, and finally Hueffer, but there is no mention of Hulme. Moreover, Aldington's thorough report of the birth of Imagism in his autobiography takes no account of Hulme's ideas (except for the business about the name, quoted above), and the three points on which the young poets decided to agree do not seem, in spite of Kermode's statement, especially Hulmian. Most claims in Hulme's favor rest upon his so-called "theory of the image," and no special influence from that is discernible in these early stirrings of the movement; in fact, the original concerns of Imagism were not theoretical at all, but disciplinary. Pound did not even make his famous definition of the Image as "presenting complexes" until well after the movement was under way, and it clearly represents his own recognition of the potentialities of "presentation" rather than an idea he began with. Nor is there reason to see Hulme's hand in the disciplines of the movement; he seems to have had almost nothing to say of use to a practicing poet. Indeed that is just where he and Pound most obviously differ.

Let us think for a moment of the difference in purposes and insights between Pound the practicing poet and Hulme the doctrinaire philosopher. It is now generally recognized that Hulme was not an original or serious thinker, nor even a literary critic. And certainly he was not a poet, although it is true that he wrote more and better poems than those in the "Complete Poetical Works." He now appears to have been a vehicle for a variety of reactionary thought along the lines of Charles Maurras and the *Action Française* group, who as Graham Hough says "did notoriously and openly what many have been willing to do covertly—used Catholic Christianity in a purely political sense, were willing to employ Christianity simply as a right-wing political weapon." Hough, as it happens, has very little respect for Hulme as a thinker: he writes of the famous essay "Romanticism and Classicism" that "words fail me to record the number of fallacies and contradictions in these twenty pages; or rather, any reasonable number of words fail; it could be done at inordinate length." With raised eyebrows Hough points out that Hulme's prophecy of a period of "dry, hard classical verse" was based on the notion of a revival of "the religious attitude," which has, as Hough notes, "produced in the past such small, dry, cheerful and sophisticated works as the *Aeneid, Dies Irae,* the *Paradiso, Piers Plowman,* and *Phèdre.*" [10] It is easy to carry this joke further: Hulme's biographer Alun Jones expounds the common notion, already quoted, that Hulme's theory of poetry finds its "most coherent expression neither in the poems of the Imagists, nor in his own poems, but in the early poetry of T. S. Eliot." Which of Eliot's early poems—*Prufrock? Portrait of a Lady? La Figlia Che Piange?*—are we going to find "small, dry, cheerful and sophisticated"? Perhaps we should go on to *The Waste Land?* Mr. Jones might at most claim some of the juvenilia. But which of even those passes Hulme's test of "this one fact: Is there any real zest in it? Did the poet have an actually realized visual object before him in which he delighted?" Again, which of Eliot's early poems uses a language that "is a compromise for a language of intuition which would hand over sensations bodily"? Which of them conforms to the principle that "the great aim is accurate, precise and definite description"? [11] Evidently there has been

[10] Graham Hough, *Image and Experience: Studies in a Literary Revolution* (Lincoln, Neb., 1960), 33–35.

[11] All three criteria are from "Romanticism and Classicism." See T. E. Hulme, *Speculations: Essays on Humanism and the Philosophy of Art,* ed. Herbert Read, first published in 1924. My source is the Harvest ed. (New York, n.d.), 132, 134, 137. Hereinafter cited as *Speculations.*

some hasty generalizing about Hulme's relevance to modernism in general and to poetry in particular.

Although Pound was affected by some of the same currents of reactionary thought, he presents nothing like Hulme's call for a revival of the "religious attitude" and "small, dry, cheerful and sophisticated verse." Nor does he seem to agree with Hulme about images, by which Hulme seems to have meant simply visual analogies. Hulme's demand for constant visualization is well known: "Each *word* must be an image *seen*, not a counter." [12] Only an ideologue could have written that. A practicing poet would have seen the obvious danger, that poetry made by that rule would very likely become picture-postcard verse. Pound was of course in favor of visual quality wherever it helped to achieve definite and precise "presentation," and often praised the visual imaginations of Dante and his other Italian and Provençal favorites. But he never pretended to believe that this was the only proper effect for poetry, and his own poetry even in its most Imagist phase shows no unusual reliance on visual effects or qualities; moreover, he continually warned his group against being "viewy" or "descriptive." The aim of Pound's Imagism was to produce a kind of pattern or structure of insight, to "present a complex instantaneously," and he never proposed to limit the means for such presentation to one sensuous effect. Quite often Pound talked about qualities of poetic form in a vocabulary derived from the plastic arts—"getting an outline," "hard-edgedness," and so on—but the values here were as often tactile as visual, since (as Donald Davie has pointed out) Pound often conceived his art in sculptural terms.[13] His historical ex-

[12] "Notes on Language and Style"; see T. E. Hulme, *Further Speculations*, ed. Sam Hynes (Lincoln, Neb., 1962), 79.

[13] See Davie, *Ezra Pound: Poet as Sculptor, passim.* Even Davie has not exhausted the evidence for Pound's thinking in these terms. For instance, he overlooks this condensation of the *ars poetica* Pound made for Iris Barry: "It is as simple as the sculptor's direction: 'Take a chisel and cut away all the stone you don't want' " (*Letters*, 91).

amples for Imagism leave no doubt that he saw it as a matter of bringing significant detail into clear, but not necessarily visual, definition: thus he uses the Wife's deafness as well as the Merchant's forked beard as examples of Imagism from Chaucer. He noted that Shakespeare often "presents something the painter does not present," as in the line, "And with the incorporal air do hold discourse," on which Pound comments, "he has made unreality indisputable." [14] Of course we may, if we wish, make a "mental picture" of such a scene; but we should remember if we do that such a phrase is only shorthand for a fairly complicated operation, involving much more than the visual sense. Any reader who tries to visualize the line from *Hamlet* will find that it contains something that is not a picture, nor yet an idea, something that partakes of both but transcends them. As I have suggested, the Image of the Imagists is an attempt to combine the essentiality of the conceptual image with the definiteness of the perceptual image; this cannot be achieved, at least not in poetry, through merely visual means. I suspect that Pound would have heartily approved Conrad's saying that his purpose in a tale was "to make you *see*," but I am sure he would have thought the phrase a reference more to insight than to sight.[15]

Visualization was not one of the points agreed on by Pound, Aldington, and H. D., but it is true that after Amy Lowell took the movement away from Pound, it degenerated: Alice Corbin Henderson, the assistant editor of *Poetry*, lamented the decline of Imagism from Pound's rigorous standards into "pictorial impression" when she reviewed the annual anthology in 1918. [16] If that is all that is understood by Imagism, then I suppose Hulme might as well have the credit. But Pound cannot be implicated in such a movement.

[14] This quotation and the historical examples are from "Imagisme and England," *T.P.'s Weekly* (February 20, 1915), 185.
[15] Joseph Conrad, Preface to *The Nigger of the "Narcissus."*
[16] "Imagism: Secular and Esoteric," *Poetry*, XI (1918), 340.

For Hulme the image was a "visual analogy"; this is a phrase
he used many times in his "Lecture on Modern Poetry" and
"Notes on Language and Style," and Alun Jones tells us that the
"chief instrument in [Hulme's] poetic synthesis is the analogy,
or metaphor, or, what Hulme consistently refers to as the
image." [17] Yet anyone who examines the poems of the 1912–14
movement carefully will agree that they are not dependent on
images in the sense of metaphors or analogies. Nor is it easy to
see why Imagism seemed so revolutionary if such a conventional
understanding was really what the poets had in mind. A comparison on this point will make clear, I believe, that the minds of
Hulme and Pound were so divergent as to be irreconcilable.
First let us see what Hulme says about analogies in a representative passage: "For example, when I say that the hill was clad
with trees, it merely conveys the fact to me that it was covered.
But the first time that expression was used by a poet, and to him
it was an image recalling to him the distinct visual analogy of a
man clad in clothes; but the image has died." [18] Actually this is
nothing more than the standard explanation for dead metaphor,
but it is the keystone of Hulme's thought, and the "distinct visual analogy" turns out to be the ultimate desideratum in his theory. In his fragmentary "Notes on Language and Style" he writes:
"Never, never, never a simple statement. It has no effect. Always
must have analogies, which make an other-world through-the-
glass effect, which is what I want." Slightly earlier analogies are
put forward as the real bases of mental activity: "Thought is
prior to language and consists in the simultaneous presentation
to the mind of two different images. . . . Thought is the joining
together of new analogies." It is predictable that the poetic problems Hulme sets himself in these notes tend to resemble this one:

[17] *Life and Opinions of T. E. Hulme,* 52.
[18] *Further Speculations,* 75. The passage apparently dates from 1908 or
1909; see Hynes's introduction, p. xviii.

"The two tarts walking along Piccadilly on tiptoe, going home, with hat on back of head. Worry until could find the exact model analogy that will reproduce the extraordinary effect they produce. Could be done at once by an artist in a blur." [19] The solution as well as the problem can be identified in one such case. In "Romanticism and Classicism" Hulme writes of the difficulty of finding the "exact epithet" for the impression "if you are walking behind a woman in the street, [and] you notice the curious way in which the skirt rebounds from her heels"; in some fragmentary poems, we find this line: "The flounced edge of skirt, recoiling like waves off a cliff." [20] Typically the solution is an analogy, or what Pound would have called an "explanatory metaphor."

Now this whole emphasis is at variance with Pound's convictions. First, he insisted that the Imagist's problem was not one of finding metaphors to explain his feelings: "Emotional force gives the image. By this I do not mean that it gives an 'explanatory metaphor'; though it might be hard to draw an exact border line between the two. We have left false metaphor, ornamental metaphor to the rhetorician." [21] Second, he seems to have a lasting distaste for analogies, and one searches almost in vain for the word "analogy," or even "metaphor" or "image" used in that sense in his writings; what discussion one finds usually is contemptuous: "You can *prove* nothing by analogy. The analogy is either range-finding or fumble." [22] Similarly, conventional ideas of metaphor bored him; in the early *Spirit of Romance*, he indicated that his interest was in "the 'language beyond metaphor,' that is, the more compressed or elliptical expression of metaphorical perception, such as antithesis

---

[19] *Further Speculations*, 87, 84, 82.
[20] *Speculations*, 136; *Further Speculations*, 217.
[21] "As for Imagisme," *New Age*, XVI (1915), 349.
[22] *ABC of Reading*, 84.

suggested or implied in verbs and adjectives." [23] This interest forecasts Imagism, with its brushing aside of ordinary "ornamental metaphor." Pound expressed his contempt for analogies more savagely in his Vorticist period, connecting them with a sterile imitative aesthetic particularly hated by the Vorticists. "The Vorticist relies not upon similarity or analogy, not upon likeness or mimicry," proclaimed Pound in *Blast*, and elsewhere he suggested that the whole mimetic, representational tradition was part of a dark conspiracy of repressive forces, "the amorphous and petrified and the copying," ranged against "the men who invent and create." [24] The idea of art as a *copy* of something or as a stylized comparison revolted the Vorticists, who insisted that it must be primary expression. In Pound's words: "The image is the poet's pigment. The painter should use his colour because he sees it or feels it. I don't much care whether he is representative or non-representative. He should *depend*, of course, on the creative, not upon the mimetic or representational part in his work. It is the same in writing poems . . . ." [25] In the terms of literary history, we might say that Pound's dictum that "emotional force gives the image" is related to Coleridge's Imagination or "esemplastic power," whereas Hulme was interested only in that arbitrary and capricious selection of analogies that constitutes Fancy: he proclaimed that "the particular weapon of this new classical spirit, when it works in verse, will be fancy. And in this I imply the superiority of fancy . . . . fancy will be superior to imagination." [26] Pound's friend May Sinclair wrote in trying to define Imagism: "I am pretty certain which of several old things it is *not*. It is not Symbolism. It has nothing to do with image-making. It abhors Imagery. Imagery is one of the old worn-out decorations the Imagists have scrapped . . . . It is

[23] In my edition (Norfolk, Conn., 1953), 158.
[24] *Blast* No. 1 (June 20, 1914), 154; *Gaudier-Brzeska*, 122.
[25] *Gaudier-Brzeska*, 86.
[26] *Speculations*, 113.

fancy, not imagination, that is concerned with symbols and with imagery." [27]

The particular doctrines that constituted Imagist discipline afford another instructive differentiation between Hulme and Pound. Hulme never came close to the idea of "living language," partly because of a hostility to language in general which I shall discuss presently. In calling for "freshness" in poetry he had no thought of idiom, daily speech, or the real language of men, which he regarded as worse than useless in poetry; rather, he meant by this "new analogies": "Plain speech is essentially inaccurate. It is only by new metaphors, that is, by fancy, that it can be made precise." [28] I can find no evidence that Hulme had ever thought enough about the matter to know what Pound or Hueffer would have meant by "living language," and the consequence was that his thinking about related problems was grotesquely old-fashioned. For example, it is widely known that Hulme called for the adaptation in English of French *vers-libre*, and some have even thought that because the Imagists required composition "in the sequence of the musical phrase, not in sequence of a metronome" that they were thereby indebted to Hulme. Leaving aside the question of why free verse should be thought Hulme's property, let us look at his rationale for its use:

Starting then from this standpoint of extreme modernism, what are the principal features of verse at the present time? It is this: that it is read and not chanted. We may set aside all theories that we read verse internally as mere verbal quibbles. We have thus two distinct arts. The one intended to be chanted, and the other intended to be read in the study. . . . I quite admit that poetry intended to be recited must be written in regular metre, but I contend that this method of recording impressions by visual images in distinct lines does not require the old metric system.[29]

[27] "Two Notes," 88–89.
[28] *Speculations*, 137.
[29] *Further Speculations*, 73.

Not only is he totally unaware of the point that free verse allows the poet to catch the real speech-rhythms, the cadences of living language, but his idea of "extreme modernism" demands what we might call closet poetry. If "what we have suffered from" is "the removal of verse from its producer and its reproducer, the voice," as Charles Olson puts it, Hulme only adds to the suffering.[30]

This deep division between Pound and Hulme extends naturally to another fundamental source of Imagist discipline, prose: "In prose as in algebra concrete things are embodied in signs or counters which are moved about according to rules, without being visualized at all in the process . . . . A poet says a ship 'coursed the seas' to get a physical image, instead of the counter word 'sailed.' Visual meanings can only be transferred by the new bowl of metaphor; prose is an old pot that lets them leak out." [31] I would like to remark first on the staleness of Hulme's example, and its inappropriateness for the purpose. Is "a ship coursed the seas" substantially more vivid than "a ship sailed?" The example indicates the remoteness of Hulme's thought from real poetic problems, as does his dogmatic antinomy between poetry and prose. Certainly Pound would have had a major quarrel with Hulme's idea that prose is inimical to poetry and hence worse than useless for the poet to study. Actually, Hulme's attitude toward prose is simply an extension of his basic hostility to language; early in his career he seems to have been badly shaken by a realization that speech can in some cases be merely reflex action. He speaks in "Romanticism and Classicism" about the experiments of a certain psychologist, who "found that in certain cases of dementia, where the people were quite

[30] *The New American Poetry: 1945–1960*, ed. Donald M. Allen (New York, 1960), 392.

[31] *Speculations*, 134–35. Wallace Martin in *"The New Age" Under Orage* says that this doctrine "we can assume was the theory [Hulme] expounded at the meetings of the forgotten school" (p. 168).

unconscious so far as the exercise of reasoning went, that very intelligent answers were given to a succession of questions on politics and such matters. The meaning of these questions could not possibly have been understood. Language here acted after the manner of a reflex." This I take it was the origin of his idea that "prose is due to a faculty of the mind something resembling reflex action in the body." [32] And it must have played an important part in fashioning what his best contemporary critic, Sam Hynes, calls "Hulme's deep distrust of words, as counters removed from the 'cinders' of reality." [33]

This "deep distrust of words" is worth examining in order to extend the distinction from Pound. Hulme had no interest in registration of reality—the whole purpose of Pound's Imagism—because he didn't believe it could be done in words. One section of "Notes on Language and Style" is called "Contempt for Language," and he calls language a "large clumsy instrument. . . . a cumbrous growth, a compound of old and new analogies." After defining thought as "the simultaneous presentation to the mind of two different images," he commented, "language is only a more or less feeble way of doing this." [34] At bottom he seems to have been what I would call a simple nominalist: "cinders" was his favorite term for an ultimately indescribable reality, and his usual metaphor for the relation of language to reality was the imposing of a "chessboard" on a heap of cinders; the Bergsonian insistence that reality was flux and was falsified by concepts led Hulme to feel that language was totally arbitrary, pure convention, mere assigned names. Pound has been accused of being a nominalist too, by some critics, but his deep and almost naïve faith in the powers of language to coalesce with reality makes this accusation ridiculous: almost any passage from *How to Read* belies it. It was not casually that he quoted Aquinas (via

[32] *Speculations*, 124; *Further Speculations*, 74.
[33] *Further Speculations*, xx.
[34] *Ibid.*, 83–85.

Dante): *"Nomina sunt consequentia rerum."* [35] Let us turn back to Hulme, whose very images for these processes betray a dreary nihilism entirely foreign to Pound's thought. "Many necessary conditions must be fulfilled before the counters and the chessboard can be posed elegantly on the cinders. Illness and death easily disturb and give falls from this condition. . . . When all is arranged the counters are moved about. This is happiness, moving to enthusiastic conclusions, the musical note, perhaps Art. But it must be largely artificial." [36] That Hulme's boosters were able to parade such stuff as serious thought is remarkable in itself, although I suppose it coincides with a shallow form of the logical positivism that was in vogue some years ago. For our purposes, that melancholy skepticism tells us why the problems of art and language were always solipsistic ones for Hulme, for it denies the possibility of objective meaning. Contrast the following passage with Pound's belief in the potentialities of language:

The great aim is accurate, precise and definite description. The first thing is to recognise how extraordinarily difficult this is. It is no mere matter of carefulness; you have to use language, and language is by its very nature a communal thing; that is, it expresses never the exact thing but a compromise—that which is common to you, me and everybody. But each man sees a little differently, and to get out clearly and exactly what he does see, he must have a terrific struggle with language, whether it be with words or the technique of other arts. [37]

Hulme is the perennial adolescent, struggling to "express" what he "really feels." It is evident that he does not mean "precise and definite description" in Pound's sense of using an accurate language, but a *subjective* process aimed at replacing language

[35] *Gaudier-Brzeska*, 92. Pound got this, of course, from the *Vita Nuova*.
[36] *Speculations*, 220.
[37] *Ibid.*, 132.

with intuitions: "Poet's mood vague and passes away, indefinable. The poem he makes selects, builds up, and makes even his own mood more definite to him." And, again, "the poet is forced to use new analogies, and especially to construct a plaster model of a thing to express his emotion at the sight of the vision he sees, his wonder and ecstasy." It is no surprise that he wanted from his analogies "an other-world through-the-glass effect" or "a sense of wonder, a sense of being united in another mystic world." [38] (Some contemporary critics have chuckled at the cloudy Romanticism underlying Hulme's attacks on Romanticism; we might compare the above desires for a mystic "otherworld" with his sneer at the Romantic idea that poetry "must lead . . . to a beyond of some kind." [39]) Pound, on the other hand, believed that poetic discipline was precisely a "matter of carefulness," and never doubted that language could express "the exact thing."

Hulme's program for poetry is for a complete divorce between art and reality. "All literature and poetry is life seen in a mirror; it must be absolutely removed from reality, and can never be attained." [40] Since it is useless to try to register reality in words, Hulme advises a naïve Romantic self-expressiveness: "Seek for the maximum of individual and personal expression," in order that "some vague mood shall be communicated." [41] For Hulme, there is nothing else for the artist to express; his famous call for the "exact curve" really refers to the contours of an individual's solipsistic thought. In short, where Pound wants to

[38] *Further Speculations*, 94, 78, 87–88.
[39] *Speculations*, 127.
[40] *Further Speculations*, 88. Cf. 89: "Must be imaginary world. Trick it out with fancies. Analogies must be substituted for what suggests something, a cloud of fancies, e.g. Waterloo Bridge in the early morning." The sense of unreality is a positive necessity, since the poet must make it obvious that his subjective analogies are "substitutes" for what external stimuli "suggest."
[41] *Further Speculations*, 71–72.

present "complexes" that register realities, Hulme wants to express his own "complexes." It may be that he was a prophet in proposing this method, but not a prophet of Imagism. "It is therefore necessary to get as large as possible change in sense impressions, cf. looking in shop windows, and war-game. The more change of shapes and sights there is the more chance of inspiration." [42] This never could be Imagism, but it may in fact be a program for a mildly surrealist poetry. The poem that stands first in the "Complete Poetical Works" is a fair sample:

> Autumn
> A touch of cold in the Autumn night—
> I walked abroad,
> And saw the ruddy moon lean over a hedge
> Like a red-faced farmer.
> I did not stop to speak, but nodded,
> And round about were the wistful stars
> With white faces like town children.

This illustrates the effect of "strangeness" for which Hulme strove. For him nothing much mattered except that the visual analogies be unusual, preferably weird.

Pound was not, of course, the first man to use the word "image." There were many reasons why he chose to call his movement "Imagisme," including perhaps the currency of the word in various circles he had frequented. Calling Hulme an "original or pre-" Imagist appears to have been one of Pound's ways of indicating a broad similarity of purpose in London groups who wanted a new mode in twentieth-century poetry. But the specific doctrines of his movement bear his personal stamp unmistakably, and there is little reason to suppose that any of his contemporaries except Hueffer added much to them. By

---

42 *Ibid.*, 84.

making Imagism a "movement" he naturally opened the door to varying definitions—Amy Lowell's conception was obviously far different from Pound's—but I cannot conceive of a definition so broad as to smooth over those very fundamental disagreements between Pound and Hulme. If I am to entertain any ill-tempered accusations of theft I certainly want to see more similarities between the "stolen" doctrines and the "originals."

If we are going to talk about that protean entity, the "Romantic Image" so well described by Frank Kermode, we will have to agree that there is a general relationship among the manifestations of it in Pound's time. Pound himself was quite clear about this; as he wrote to René Taupin: "l'idée de l'image doit 'quelque chose' aux symbolistes français via T. E. Hulme, via Yeats<Symons<Mallarmé. Comme le pain doit quelque chose au vanneur de blé, etc." [43] Pound's words suggest, and Kermode's analysis clearly shows, that "the image" in general was a creature of the whole ambience, not of any specific individual. In any case such a generalized entity was not the precipitating or determinative factor for the Imagist Movement, which made use of the "Romantic Image" for Pound's highly specialized purposes.

To be sure, Pound always saw Hulme as a valuable friend and ally. He regretted Hulme's death in the war, and afterwards praised him as much as he honestly could. Probably they did in the early days feel themselves to be comrades-in-arms; there prevailed then a conspiratorial sense of undermining Philistine positions on many fronts. Yet, in the end, we can find between them few profound ideological agreements; both were influenced by anti-liberalism, but I am in complete accord with Sam Hynes's conclusion that "the politics of T. S. Eliot seem to me a more logical development of Hulme's ideas than the politics of

---

[43] *Letters*, 218. I have silently corrected "Yeat" to "Yeats" and "come" to "comme."

Pound." [44] Most important, Pound's poetics suggests the possibility of a "poetry of reality," whereas Hulme's leads only to a subjective, self-assertive toying with unsatisfactory, untrustworthy words: poetry "absolutely removed from reality."

FENOLLOSA

The most thought-provoking and helpful short critique of Imagism that I know has not been given much attention in histories of the movement: it is May Sinclair's note printed in the *Egoist* in 1915. She first brought Pound and Hueffer together, and may have known something about what they were trying to do. In the note she uses H. D.'s work for illustration, but her real reference is clearly to Pound's ideas; she claimed to have known Pound's poems by heart even before the first Imagist anthology appeared. Therefore her statements have a peculiar authority. Here is the kernel of her thought: "The Image is not a substitute; it does not stand for anything but itself. Presentation not Representation is the watchword of the school. . . . You cannot distinguish between the thing and its image." She grasps the important technical point that "the passion, the emotion or the mood is never given as an abstraction," but emphasizes the conception of a poetry that does not merely describe reality but coalesces with it; she ends the essay by comparing the Imagists to believers in transubstantiation: "For them the bread and wine are the body and the blood." [45]

[44] *Further Speculations,* xxxi.

[45] "Two Notes," 88–89. Douglas Goldring (*South Lodge,* p. 39) says May Sinclair introduced Pound and Hueffer. Images indistinguishable from things takes us farther than ever, of course, from the old or ordinary senses of the word "image," hence farther from Hulme. Pound's particular friends, who knew of Imagism through him, took pains to assert that the old senses were misleading. Cf. Jean de Bosschère, "Ezra Pound," *Egoist,* IV (1917), 27: "He is free and without rhetoric—no one more so. His vision is direct; he does not use the image, but shows the things themselves with power. This is indeed a quality of the *Imagistes.*"

Here we have, I submit, the key to the more theoretical aspect of Imagism, after the phase of Imagism as discipline (or what Pound called "Imagism as a critical movement") was thoroughly established. It reflects Pound's insistence that his Image was more than an ornament or an explanatory metaphor or an analogy. He evidently reacted violently against the definition of *symbol* that seems almost inevitably to prevail in English: a substitute, a representation or signifier of some preconceived entity. We know, for instance, that he carelessly misrepresented the Symbolists in order to attack it:

Imagisme is not symbolism. The symbolists dealt in "association," that is, in a sort of allusion, almost of allegory. They degraded the symbol to the status of a word. They made it a form of metonomy [*sic*]. One can be grossly "symbolic," for example, by using the term "cross" to mean "trial."

. . . .

Almost anyone can realize that to use a symbol *with an ascribed or intended meaning* is, usually, to produce very bad art. We all remember crowns, and crosses, and rainbows, and what not in atrociously mumbled colour.[46]

This passage, and this whole side of Imagism, were products of the Vorticist redefinitions of Imagism; May Sinclair's note also postdates the earlier phase, which ended with the "Amygist" revolt of 1914. From that time on Pound had no way to enforce the disciplines he had worked out, and turned to aesthetic theory to validate and extend what he had done. The Vorticists' hatred of imitative art and their insistence on primary expression would of course have helped toward the idea of the image as real and autonomous, not merely representational. But the best help that Pound received in confirming his belief in the image was the aesthetic theory found in Ernest Fenollosa's "Essay on the Chi-

---

[46] *Gaudier-Brzeska*, 84–86.

nese Written Character." In this essay are drawn together insights that furnished Pound with persuasive evidence.

Most critics have thought that Fenollosa's important gift to Pound was the "ideogrammic method," yet Pound's early outbursts of praise for Fenollosa single out not that but Fenollosa's thesis that verbs are the basis of living language. In 1916 Pound described the essay for a young disciple:

> You should have a chance to see Fenollosa's big essay on verbs, mostly on verbs. Heaven knows when I shall get it printed. He inveighs against "IS," wants transitive verbs. "Become" is as weak as "is." Let the grime *do* something to the leaves. "All nouns come from verbs." To primitive man, a thing only IS what it *does*. That is Fenollosa, but I think the theory is a very good one for poets to go by.[47]

Indisputably the essay spends far more time on verbs than on ideograms *per se*. Fenollosa professed to believe that verbs underlie all parts of speech, even pronouns, and that only ossification of language obscures this: Chinese fortunately shows us the original state, for "the great number of these ideographic roots carry in them a *verbal idea of action*." [48] Obviously Fenollosa had the idea that primitive languages were close to nature; no doubt he imbibed Emerson at Harvard, and this Romantic primitivism can be found in "Nature" and in "The Poet," with strands linking back to Shelley's "Defence of Poetry" and beyond. "Poetry only does consciously what the primitive races

---

[47] *Letters*, 82.

[48] The essay was first printed in the *Little Review* in 1919, then in *Instigations of Ezra Pound* (New York, 1920), then separately in 1936 and 1951. It has also been reprinted in Karl Shapiro's *Prose Keys to Modern Poetry* (New York, Evanston, and London, 1962). Because of this variety of texts, and because the essay is short and my references to it numerous, I have omitted page citations and have assumed that the interested reader will want to verify not only the quotations but their contexts by reading the whole essay. (The fact that Fenollosa was wrong about Chinese has of course nothing to do with my argument.)

did unconsciously," wrote Fenollosa. In his view reality is faithfully described only by transitive verbs, for it consists entirely of actions and processes: "A true noun, an isolated thing, does not exist in nature. Things are only the terminal points, or rather the meeting points of actions, cross-sections cut through actions, snap-shots. Neither can a pure verb, an abstract motion, be possible in nature. The eye sees noun and verb as one: things in motion, motion in things, and so the Chinese conception tends to represent them." As for parts of speech, he says, "the verb must be the primary fact of nature, since motion and change are all that we can recognize in her." If the verb is primary, other parts are derived from it: Pound quotes in his letter a version of Fenollosa's dictum that "a noun is originally 'that which does something,' that which performs the verbal action." Fenollosa agreed that in a sentence like "farmer pounds rice," we have two words acting as nouns: "But in themselves, apart from this sentence-function, they are naturally verbs. The farmer is one who tills the ground, and the rice is a plant which grows in a special way."

Similarly, the other parts of speech are peeled back to reveal verbs underneath. "Even with us, to-day, we can still watch participles passing over into adjectives. . . . quality is only a power of action regarded as having an abstract inherence. Green is only a certain rapidity of vibration, hardness a degree of tenseness in cohering." These examples are arguable, but later ones are more persuasive: "In Chinese the preposition is frankly a verb, specially used in a generalized sense. . . . Thus in Chinese: By=to cause; to=to fall toward; in=to remain, to dwell; from=to follow; and so on." And for conjunctions: "Because=to use; and=to be included under one; another form of 'and'=to be parallel; or=to partake; if=to let one do, to permit." Even pronouns, in Fenollosa's analysis, "yield up their striking secrets of verbal metaphor." The implication in the essay is that we should in our usage try to recapture a sense of this verbal substratum in all the parts of speech. Fenollosa seems to have convinced Pound that if we will recognize the true verbal basis of language, we can write a poetry that will attain the desired closeness to nature.

If verbs speak the truth of nature, then great poetry from the past should depend on them. Fenollosa resorted to a sure-fire example: "I had to discover for myself why Shakespeare's English was so immeasurably superior to all others. I found that it was his persistent, natural, and magnificent use of hundreds of transitive verbs. Rarely will you find an 'is' in his sentences." For Fenollosa the copula was part of the "discredited, or rather the useless, logic of the middle ages," in which the concrete actions and processes of nature were reified into "mere particulars," "pawns," with the different classes of these connected merely by copulas, positive or negative. He suspected that we suffer from a debased form of an idea popular in the Middle Ages, that beings were arranged in hierarchies or pyramids and the most abstract entities—those at the tops of the pyramids—were the most real:

At the base of the pyramid lie *things*, but stunned, as it were. They can never know themselves for things until they pass up and down among the layers of the pyramids. The way of passing up and down the pyramid may be exemplified as follows: We take a concept of lower attenuation, such as "cherry"; we see that it is contained under one higher, such as "redness." Then we are permitted to say in sentence form, "Cherryness is contained under redness," or for short, "(the) cherry is red." If, on the other hand, we do not find our chosen subject under a given predicate we use the [negative] copula and say, for example, "(The) cherry is not liquid."

Fenollosa's criticism comes down to the principle that such predication is no predication at all, but mere linkage and comparison; it misses the active, vital force of "transferences of power" in nature, and the truths of real but not necessarily logical relationships. To better define the true form of predication, Fenollosa attacked the traditional definitions of the sentence-form. Rejecting the criterion of "a complete thought" because "in nature there is *no* completeness," he went on to denounce the usual "subject-predicate" definition as hopelessly subjective:

In the second definition of the sentence, as "uniting a subject and a predicate," the grammarian falls back on pure subjectivity. *We* do it all; it is a little private juggling between our right and left hands. The subject is that about which *I* am going to talk; the predicate is that which *I* am going to say about it. The sentence according to this definition is not an attribute of nature but an accident of man as a conversational animal.
  If it were really so, then there could be no possible test of the truth of a sentence. Falsehood would be as specious as verity. Speech would carry no conviction.

It is amazing that this passage has received so little attention from critics; perhaps the Johnsonian use of *specious* has thrown them off. For here Fenollosa proposes nothing less than a way across the terrifying Cartesian gap between internal and external, between subjective and objective; it proceeds from the conviction that we can have a truly objective predication that will manifest the operations of reality itself. The sentence-form is not an arbitrary convention, but a structural representation of these operations: "agent—act—object." "The sentence form was forced upon primitive men by nature itself. It was not we who made it; it was a reflection of the temporal order in causation. All truth has to be expressed in sentences because all truth is the *transference of power*." Transitive verbs, by predicating objectively, express reality; copulas, by suggesting that a speaker is merely manipulating concepts (as in "cherryness is contained under redness," or "the cherry is red"), obscure it. "The moment we use the copula, the moment we express subjective inclusions, poetry evaporates," because the sense of reality is diffused. The predication seems to come from us instead of the thing itself, and is reduced to "an accident of man as a conversational animal." In a true sentence, on the other hand, subject and predicate are simply aspects of a unitary process. "The true formula for thought is: The cherry tree is all that it does. Its correlated verbs compose it."

Pound must have seen this thesis about predication as the means to achieve the objectivity toward which "presentation" strives: "It means constatation of fact. It presents. It does not comment. It is irrefutable." "Comment," and the detested "rhetoric" too, are equivalents of Fenollosa's "pure subjectivity," the idea that predication consists of "what *I* am going to say about it." Presentative predication, unlike "comment," is not self-assertive and is irrefutable in that sense: the poet nothing affirmeth, and therefore never lieth. In several places Pound remarked "I agree with John Yeats on the relation of beauty to certitude"; now Fenollosa had showed him the rationale for this relation.[49] On this point Pound is at the furthest remove from Hulme, who despaired of expressing reality in words and whose poetics therefore consists almost entirely of ways of making subjective "comment."

This conception of predication helps us to understand everything else in Fenollosa's essay, including the overdiscussed ideogrammic method. The ideogram is usually understood as a mere juxtaposition of particulars held together in a vaguely analogic relationship: even Pound tended to talk this way when he was trying to explain it very simply, as in his *ABC of Reading*. In

[49] See *Literary Essays*, 13 and 284. The elder Yeats's point is evidently related to that of his son, that "you can refute Hegel but not the Saint or the Song of Sixpence." See *The Letters of W. B. Yeats*, ed. Allan Wade (New York, 1954), 922. The modern anti-rhetorician seems to see Hell as a "universe of discourse," that is, of endless argument with no certainty.

this view it simply accords with the modernist tradition of non-predication or nondiscursiveness. But Fenollosa's ideograms do make predications of the objective kind, and the great majority of his examples are *not* mere juxtapositions of particulars, but express vital and definite relationships between the elements: "In this process of compounding, two things added together do not produce a third thing but suggest some fundamental relation between them. For example, the ideograph for a 'mess-mate' is a man and a fire." It is important to notice that a man and a fire are not analogous, nor "related" like members of a family or like constituents of one of Fenollosa's "pyramids of particulars": if we don't see this, we are back in the trap of thinking of relationship as simply a form of copulative predication. When the signs for *man* and *fire* are combined, each does something to the other, predicates something, so that the essence of a new reality is manifested (not as a third thing, a "manfire" or whatever they might add up to), a new reality that inheres in the relationship. Fenollosa concluded that "relations are more real and more important than the things which they relate." More processes than states, these relationships are generally active and predicative: this is made clear in several of Fenollosa's examples, notably in "the sun sign tangled in the branches of the tree sign=east." *East* is a locus of the interaction of two vital processes, sun and tree, which "do" things to each other: sun modified by tree, tree modified by sun, form a complex. Perhaps the clearest exemplification is in Fenollosa's discussion of an ideogram that became something of a signature for Pound:

The Chinese have one word, *ming* or *mei*. Its ideograph is the sign of the sun together with the sign of the moon. It serves as verb, noun, adjective. Thus you write literally, "the sun and moon of the cup" for "the cup's brightness." Placed as a verb, you write "the cup sun-and-moons," actually "cup sun-and-moon," or in a weakened thought, "is like sun," i.e., shines. . . .

Every written Chinese word is properly just such an underlying word. . . . not something which is neither noun, verb, or adjective, but something that is all of them at once and at all times.

This suggests the fascinating possibility that the elements of poems may act as verbs for each other. Is it not more illuminating to say that the second line of the *Metró* poem ("Petals on a wet, black bough") acts as some sort of predication about the first line ("The apparition of these faces in the crowd") than as a mere analogy of it? In the "East" ideogram, *tree* modifies *sun* not in an adjectival way but in a verbal way: it does not describe the sun but extends meaning to it, or from it, by implying a relationship. So in the poem one line "says something" about the other, makes a predication, or, "in a weakened thought," an analogy.

This is a speculative line of thought, but it can be supported from observations in very different contexts. For example, that no-nonsense critic W. K. Wimsatt, Jr., states in discussing "elegant variation":

Predicates of propositions are not the only parts that have a predicative function. Almost all terms in a discourse manage to betray some predication, to assert something of something. "The barn is big. It is red." "Barn" predicates as much as and more than "big" and "red". . . . "Much-enduring noble Odysseus heard him not". . . . What looks like a heavily weighted subject, all that comes before the assertion or copula, may turn out to be more of a predicate than what comes after.[50]

If we follow this line, the world may begin to look like an infinite source of predications. Language may become more active and alive. Poetry, perhaps, becomes valuable for its sense of movement, for the way in which it can capture vital *process*. This is possibly the line of thought Pound was following when

[50] W. K. Wimsatt, Jr., "When is Variation 'Elegant'?" *The Verbal Icon: Studies in the Meaning of Poetry* (New York, 1958), 189.

he wrote: "The defect of earlier imagist propaganda was not in misstatement but in incomplete statement. The diluters took the handiest and easiest meaning, and thought only of the STA-TIONARY image. If you can't think of imagism or phanopoeia as including the moving image, you will have to make a really needless division of fixed image and praxis or action." [51] It is worth noting that Pound made this observation in the process of commenting on a "moving image" from Scandinavian saga: "Skarpheddin's jump and slide on the ice, and the meeting of Grettir, or whoever it was, with the bear do not fade from one's memory. You can't believe it is fiction. Some Icelander on a ledge must at some time have saved himself by lopping off the outside paw of a bear, and so making the brute lose its balance. This is in a sense phanopoeia, the throwing of an image on the mind's retina." The permanence of such images depends not on witty comparison nor even on a vivid picture: although Pound wrote "mind's retina," if the image is not to fade from one's memory it must have the "shock and stroke" of experience, must be felt rather than merely seen, and must embody a kinetic sense of movement; purely visual images, for all their utility, tend to be rather static. Memorability is enhanced by the sense of action or process to which Fenollosa referred, a more than visual sense; capturing that sense, the image becomes so real "you can't believe it is fiction," or "you can't distinguish between the thing and its image." Pound is his own illustration: the work itself has receded so far that he can't be sure who is involved, but the image retains its vividness.

Objective predication, with its aim of capturing such "moving images," is the key to Pound's idea of a "poetry of reality" and to Pound's work as a whole. For Pound is, in Charles Tomlinson's phrase, "engaged with the 'out-there' "; the remark is in a review of Donald Davie's *Ezra Pound: Poet as Sculptor*, which

[51] *ABC of Reading*, 52.

makes the same point at length in a discussion of the chthonic wasp in Canto LXXXIII.[52] As Davie says, "At no point does the wasp become a symbol for something in Pound's predicament, or for his ethical or other programs, or for his personality. The wasp retains its otherness as an independent form of life; it is only by doing so that it can be a source of comfort." Davie contrasts Pound to "any man whose main interest in the external world is as a repertoire of objective correlatives for his own states of mind"; as a criticism of Eliot this is unfair, but it could well characterize the differences between Pound and Hulme.[53] The wasp's reality is embodied in lines whose clearness and precision come not from the attempt to describe exactly the poet's own feelings on seeing the wasp, but from the technique, by then second nature with Pound, of letting the thing "say itself" —letting it be, like Fenollosa's cherry tree, "all that it does." Even more remarkable from the point of view of poetics, Pound has such confidence in this method that he has no anxiety about "refining himself out of existence" or achieving "impersonality," so he appears in his own poems with ease and freedom; this gives him a tremendous flexibility. The principle at issue is described by another highly personal but nonsubjective poet, Charles Olson, in terms of the poet's relation to objects:

Objectism is the getting rid of the lyrical interference of the individual as ego, of the "subject" and his soul, that peculiar presumption by which western man has interposed himself between what he is as a creature of nature (with certain instructions to carry out) and those other creations of nature which we may, with no derogation, call objects. . . . But if he stays inside himself, if he is contained within his nature as he is participant in the larger force, he will be able to listen, and his hearing through himself will give him secrets objects share.[54]

[52] Charles Tomlinson, "The Tone of Pound's Critics," *Agenda*, IV (October–November, 1965), 48.
[53] Davie, *Ezra Pound: Poet as Sculptor*, 176–77.
[54] Olson, "Projective Verse," 395.

Real art comes from the self and bears the stamp of its maker everywhere, but this does not mean that he projects his personality all over the place, nor does he reduce everything, in a fit of queasy solipsistic doubt, to his own inner vaguenesses. The test for a poet, as Olson sees, "lies in how he conceives his relation to nature, that force to which he owes his somewhat small existence." Pound passes. A good many other poets pass also, having similarly achieved a style that is personal but not subjective, and many have anticipated Pound in the use of himself as a *persona*. But in Pound's work the paradox is perhaps sharper than anywhere else. It was Charles Norman, who as a biographer cannot have made such a statement lightly, who asserted that the *Cantos* form the "most autobiographical poem in the English language"; but what do we know of the private Pound or of his subjectivity when we have read the poem? [55] The *Cantos* give me no feeling of knowing "Pound the man" while reading; if autobiography, it is that of a reagent in history who tests what he comes into contact with. Most of the hostile criticism has complained that not enough subjective "order" is imposed. Disturbed by the idea of bits and pieces of reality predicating themselves, the critics have demanded that Pound "comment," say more as himself, develop a philosophy and elaborate it in verse. Actually Pound talks incessantly in his poem, of course, but somehow it isn't the kind of subjective "what I have to say about it" that we are used to.

The sharpness of the paradox in Pound's work is almost certainly related to a comment once made by Hueffer: "The Impressionist author is sedulous to avoid letting his personality appear in the course of his book. On the other hand, his whole book, his whole poem is merely an expression of his personality." A self-indulgent author might use that principle to pour himself all over his work under a thin disguise, but Pound would not

55 *Ezra Pound*, 335.

have put it to that use. Here is his adaptation: "The artist seeks out the luminous detail and presents it. He does not comment. His work remains the permanent basis of psychology and metaphysics." [56] This was written before he read Fenollosa, but it shows how the Imagist discipline of "presentation" was preparing him to become a faithful believer in the power of objective predication.

The subjective-objective dichotomy is an old chestnut among problems in poetics, to be sure. Today a poet is likely to cross the great gap without even looking down, as William Carlos Williams did. But Pound had more failures to instruct him than successes; the obvious example is Coleridge, who asserted the interpenetration of mind and reality by figuring imaginative perception as "a repetition in the finite mind of the eternal act of creation in the infinite I AM." [57] Unfortunately, assertions that man "creates" his world can be construed as relativist and then solipsist platitudes—"each man sees a little differently," as Hulme said, and then follows the doubt as to whether objective reality exists at all. The nineteenth century was too dominated by the subjectivist momentum inherent in idealism and expressionism to be a good time to break this chain of thought. Hence no one except Fenollosa could show Pound the way to validate his instinctive feelings on this matter. Fenollosa's solution yields a world not of static objects with meaning imposed on them but a drama of meanings unfolding from actions and processes. It has certain resemblances to the organic universe of Alfred North Whitehead.

The problem comes up in a different way when we get to metaphor and analogy. Analogy can be revealing, but its basis, likeness, tends to be reductive as predication. Moreover it limits

[56] Hueffer, *Critical Writings*, 43; Pound, "A Rather Dull Introduction," *New Age*, X (1911), 130.
[57] Samuel Taylor Coleridge, *Biographia Literaria*, Chap. Eight.

the realm of poetic activity: if analogy is all there is to metaphor, then the poet merely picks and chooses among likenesses by an "arbitrary subjective process." Coleridge called this operation "Fancy." He knew there was more to poetry than that; so did Fenollosa:

The primitive metaphors do not spring from arbitrary subjective processes. They are possible only because they follow objective lines of relations in nature herself. Relations are more real and more important than the things which they relate. The forces which produce the branch-angles of an oak lay potent in the acorn. . . . This is more than analogy, it is identity of structure. Nature furnishes her own clues. Had the world not been full of homologies, sympathies, and identities, thought would have been starved and language chained to the obvious. There would have been no bridge whereby to cross from the minor truth of the seen to the major truth of the unseen.

Metaphor must be "more than analogy," and must present more than "the minor truth of the seen," for "the greater part of natural truth is hidden in processes too minute for vision and in harmonies too large, in vibrations, cohesions and in affinities." Fenollosa's emphasis was on the relations formed by things making predications of each other; therefore he defined metaphor as "the use of material images to suggest immaterial relations."

More and more the simplistic idea that resemblance is the basis of metaphor appears unsatisfactory today. Charles Feidelson, writing of American literature from a post-Symbolist point of view, feels this dissatisfaction and takes the line that "resemblance is a function of logical, not metaphoric, structure." He expands this into a conclusion that might well suit Fenollosa:

Marvell's phrase, "the iron gates of life," does not "point out" or "play on" a pre-existing similarity between the logical elements, life and iron gates. It is not sufficient to add, as does Richards, that the relation between "tenor" and "vehicle" is "even more the work of their unlikenesses than of their likenesses." The phrase, taken as a whole, establishes the idea of life *under the aspect of* iron gates, and of iron gates under the aspect of life. If emphasis is laid upon "iron gates," the phrase "of life" serves to place "iron gates" in a certain light; and if emphasis is laid upon "life," the phrase "iron gates" compels a special meaning upon it [i.e., predicates something of it]. From this standpoint, both the similarities and the differences between tenor and vehicle become irrelevant. . . . The elements of a metaphor have meaning only by virtue of the whole which they create by their interaction; a metaphor presents parts that do not fully exist until the whole which they themselves produce comes into existence.[58]

The conclusion especially is almost a restatement of Fenollosa's thesis about ideograms. Of his chosen example Feidelson states "the *real* tenor is a meaning produced by the interaction of the two terms, which together form the vehicle." This is as much as to say that the tenor is a relationship, as Fenollosa had: "In this process of compounding, two things added together do not produce a third thing but suggest some fundamental relation between them." His example was the sign for *mess-mate:* man plus fire. These are no more alike than iron gates and life, but when seen in relation suggest the meaning.

Apart from artists of the sensitivity of Henry James, who remarked in the preface to *Roderick Hudson* that the novelist's subject is "the related state, to each other, of certain figures and things," no one could have placed a higher value on relationships than Fenollosa—or Pound after him, who would have appreciated the correlation between these two. For if Fenollosa's world is one of process, it is also one in which relations themselves are kinds of processes. "Immaterial relations" embodied in metaphors are always at work, interpreting the world: "Metaphor, the revealer of nature, is the very substance of poetry. The known interprets the obscure, the universe is alive with myth."

[58] Charles Feidelson, Jr., *Symbolism and American Literature* (Chicago, 1953), 59–60.

It follows that neither metaphor nor myth is a mere poetic pastime, but an apprehension of the vital universe in the most meaningful way. As a matter of fact Pound developed a view of myth on exactly those lines, as I shall discuss later. His statement on myth is just where Fenollosa's thought seems to cohere: the derivation of myth from metaphor makes his analysis of language relevant to poetry in general, and verbs bind all the elements together: myth, poetry, relation, predication, image—all are dependent on that sense of activity and process that makes the verb the primary unit of language. The sense of reality in any of these things comes from their approaching "a vivid shorthand picture of the operations of nature."

This synthesis of thought, for all the significance it had to Pound, only brings to bear in an articulate way the whole thrust of Imagism toward the same problems. Pound groped toward a poetry of reality in "Prolegomena," where he stated that the new poetry's force "will lie in its truth, its interpretative power"; in a footnote he appended to Fenollosa's essay Pound used the interpreting function to clarify his old distinction between "true metaphor that is interpretative metaphor, or image, as diametrically opposed to untrue, or ornamental metaphor." The distinction, plainly, was between metaphors that are objective predications along the "lines of force" of nature, and those that arise from a poet's desire to decorate his poem. This is substantiated in one of his prior discussions to which Pound directs us in another footnote to Fenollosa:

The point of Imagisme is that it does not use images *as ornaments*. The image is itself the speech. The image is the word beyond formulated language.

I once saw a small child go to an electric light switch and say, "Mamma, can I *open* the light?" She was using the age-old language of exploration, the language of art. It was a sort of metaphor, but she was not using it as ornamentation.[59]

---

[59] *Gaudier-Brzeska*, 88.

The child's words follow "objective lines of relations in nature herself." The known interprets the obscure.

In yet another way Pound moved toward Fenollosa's idea of objective predication with his dictum that "the natural object is always the *adequate* symbol"; the poet should not have to impose a superadded meaning. The logical result of this ambition was Aldington's formulation for Imagism: "We convey an emotion by presenting the object and circumstance of that emotion without comment. . . . we present that woman, we make an 'Image' of her, we make the scene convey the emotion." The woman is made to "reveal herself." That is the idea of objective predication without Fenollosa's theoretical underpinning.

Pound foreshadows Fenollosa in several other areas: his call for a "language beyond metaphor" anticipates Fenollosa's demonstration that metaphor is "more than analogy," for instance. But the most comprehensive demonstration of their fundamental affinity can be found in comparing Pound's Imagist principle that a few words should be made to carry a great burden of meaning with Fenollosa's characterization of the essence of poetry: "Poetic thought works by suggestion, crowding maximum meaning into the single phrase pregnant, charged, and luminous from within." Pound much later wrote a definition that contains more than an echo of Fenollosa's sentence: "Great literature is simply language charged with meaning to the utmost possible degree." [60] Thus did Fenollosa underwrite what is perhaps the most basic of Pound's poetic principles, a principle for which Pound later began to use a succinct motto taken from a German-Italian dictionary: *Dichten = condensare.*

It should be emphasized that Fenollosa's demand for verbs has nothing to do with a "vigorous" poetry; he did not desire a sense

---

[60] *Literary Essays*, 23. By Pound's "foreshadowing" or "anticipation" of Fenollosa, I mean of course that Imagism was constructed before Pound had read the essay.

of life and activity for its own sake, but because images with such a sense were conducive to the interpenetration of language and reality. If we attain that sense of liveness that comes with things "saying themselves," we not only capture nature in motion but get rid of the "subjective inclusions" that the copula suggests. The verb "is," tending to place the locus of predication in the speaker who makes the connection, marks a degenerating sense of language:

We do not say a tree "greens itself," but "the tree is green"; not that "monkeys bring forth live young," but that "the monkey is a mammal." This is an ultimate weakness of language. It has come from generalizing all intransitive words into one. As "live," "see," "walk," "breathe," are generalized into states by dropping their objects, so these weak verbs are in turn reduced to the abstractest state of all, namely, bare existence.

There is in reality no such verb as a pure copula, no such original conception, our very word *exist* means "to stand forth," to show oneself by a definite act. "Is" comes from the Aryan root *as*, to breathe. "Be" is from *bhu*, to grow.

Fenollosa thus insists on epiphanic manifestation as the condition for existence: the thing stands forth, exists, only by doing something; and it is up to poetry to make use of living language and true metaphor to indicate the "immaterial relations" that allow us to apprehend what at bottom these unique acts or processes are. Poetry must create a set of relations among words that epiphanizes such an act, must register an image of a thing so active and alive that "you cannot distinguish between the thing and its image." That phrase, as I have tried to make clear, is not a call for *trompe l'oeil* effects, but for a poetry of transubstantiation, for the real presence in the symbolic medium.

THREE

POUND AND JOYCE

The Universal in the Particular

THE TANG OF REALITY

O F ALL POUND'S remarkable literary friendships, that with James Joyce is perhaps the most difficult to account for. He had been attracted to Yeats by reputation, and in Eliot he saw a hope of the long-desired American Risorgimento in letters. Other friendships had other explainable rationales. But no immediate cause explains his instinctive understanding and enthusiasm for the work of an unknown Irishman, from whom he was sundered by temperament, mode of life, literary background, and, during the first years of their acquaintance, by Joyce's virtual internment on the Continent during the war. They did not meet in person until years after Pound had performed now-familiar prodigies of getting Joyce's work into print, arranging for his support, and so on. Moreover, Pound proclaimed Joyce's genius to the world not on the basis of the Herculean labors of *Ulysses* or *A Portrait*, but soon after he had detected the promise in *Chamber Music* and *Dubliners* (though it is true he got to see the first chapter of the *Portrait* at the same time).[1] Pound's consistently amazing instinct for genius in this case did more than disprove that "No one knows, at sight, a masterpiece," but saw even in the lesser work the talent and discipline that would produce the masterpiece.

Pound's appreciation of Joyce's prose is perhaps easiest to understand. "As Madox Ford had been preaching the virtues of the french prose, of what he called impressionist prose, for some years, and as the Imagist FIRST manifesto had demanded 'Direct treatment of the THING whether subjective or objective, and the use of NO WORD that did not contribute to the presentation,' a few people recognized the significance of Joyce's first prose book at once." This was from a comment Pound made many years later; he wrote in 1914, "Mr. Joyce writes a clear hard prose. . . . I can lay down a good piece of French writing and pick up a piece of writing by Mr. Joyce without feeling as if my head were being stuffed through a cushion." Manifestly it was Hueffer's lessons in the "prose tradition" that prepared Pound to recognize the value of Joyce's style in the "unspeakably difficult art" of good prose; Pound indicated as much by comparing Joyce to the good impressionists, "whose forerunner was Stendhal and whose founder was Flaubert," who "deal in exact presentation" and who have been "perhaps the most beneficial force in modern writing." Given what such phrases meant to Pound's own art, this was high tribute. But he also indicated that Joyce went further than these impressionists; by excluding "all unnecessary detail," he suggested, Joyce might be able to achieve that "intensity, selection, and concentration" which the impressionists too often lacked. Pound similarly saw Imagism advancing upon impressionist achievements through more rigid discipline; so it was not a whim that he accepted a Joyce poem for the anthology *Des Imagistes*. Even then it must have been

[1] For the biographical details see Richard Ellmann, *James Joyce* (New York, 1959), 360–66, 491–95, etc. But note Ellmann's repetition of the myth about Hulme and Imagism.

possible to see from Joyce's style that he had the dedication required for Imagist or even more rigorous disciplines. Pound was not disappointed in this expectation, and continued to nominate Joyce as the new incumbent of the "prose tradition"; when *Ulysses* appeared, he wrote that "Joyce has taken up the art of writing where Flaubert left it." [2]

Important as prose style was, the affinity between these two suggests that there was more to it than that. As prose discipline signified for Pound a means toward a sweeping reform of poetry, so his apprehension of Joyce's merits seems to have been a sign of a further goal: it is almost as if Joyce showed him the way to put twentieth-century literature on a basis not only technically sound, but metaphysically solid. One theme recurs in Pound's essays on Joyce aside from praise of stylistic achievements: fascination with the way Joyce had been able to use a narrow, insular city to imply the world in general.

> He gives us Dublin as it presumably is. He does not descend to farce. He does not rely upon Dickensian caricature. He gives us things as they are, not only for Dublin but for every city. Erase the local names and a few specifically local allusions, and a few historic events of the past, and substitute a few different local names, allusions and events, and these stories could be retold of any town.
> That is to say, the author is quite capable of dealing with things about him, and dealing directly, yet these details do not engross him, he is capable of getting at the universal element beneath them. . . . Good writing, good presentation can be specifically local, but it must not depend on locality. Mr. Joyce does not present "types" but individuals. I mean he deals with common emotions which run through all races. He does not bank on "Irish character." [3]

2 The first quotation in the paragraph is from "Past History," *English Journal*, coll. ed., XXII (1933), 352. For the 1914 essay, see note 68 to Chap. One, and *Literary Essays*, 399–402; the review of *Ulysses* first appeared in the *Dial* in 1922, and see *Literary Essays*, 403.

3 *Literary Essays*, 401.

To have pinched, provincial Dublin suggest the great world was noteworthy enough, but in Pound's eyes this was not a mere artful device. He lingered on the means Joyce used to evoke Dublin only in order to point out that something far more consequential than "local colour" was going on, and implied that these means took Joyce near the very nature of reality—not so much that Dublin was a "microcosm," but rather that it was potentially any other particular locus: Molly Bloom, he said, "exists presumably in Patagonia as she exists in Jersey City or Camden." [4] He stressed the philosophic implication in his phrase "universal element," in an essay on Eliot: "James Joyce has written the best novel of my decade, and perhaps the best criticism of it has come from a Belgian who said, 'All this is as true of my country as of Ireland.' Eliot has a like ubiquity of application. Art does not avoid universals, it strikes at them all the harder in that it strikes through particulars." [5] In short, Pound believed that Joyce, and Eliot too, had attained a "poetry of reality" that not only answered the call of "presentation" for an exact proportion between detail and insight, but embodied a metaphysical world of universal meanings. The formula for such a relation between literature and reality was one that would have pleased a Schoolman of the Moderate Realist persuasion: *universalia in rebus*.

Critics of Pound ignore his statement of belief in universals to their cost. So convenient has it been to explain Pound away as a "nominalist" that many have mistaken his attack on "abstractions" as a nihilistic rejection of universals. They are therefore nonplussed when Pound says that the *Cantos* contain "magic moments or moments of metamorphosis" that lead into a "divine or permanent world," [6] and are unable to see the full implications of these lines:

[4] *Ibid.*, 407.
[5] "T. S. Eliot," *Poetry*, X (1917), 267; *Literary Essays*, 420.
[6] *Letters*, 210. Although he largely rejected Symbolist aesthetic after

                            as says Aristotle
        philosophy is not for young men
        their *Katholou* can not be sufficiently derived from
              their *hekasta*
        their generalities cannot be born from a sufficient phalanx
                                                      of particulars
                                                  (Canto LXXIV)

They reckon without the obvious meaning of his attitude toward the interpenetration of language and reality, and his belief
that the health of a society depends on the exactness of its language. How could a nominalist call for exactness in language?
If language is merely a behavioristic convention, an arbitrary
assigning of names, words cannot possibly have precise meanings or exactly define things. Pound himself is responsible, it is
true, for some of the loose repetitions about "ideogrammic
method" and "method of science" that have contributed to the
impression that he is a nominalist, but that does not lessen the
duty of exact criticism to get the facts straight.

---

the early period of Yeatsian influence (see Chap. One), Pound sometimes
verged on what may seem a Symbolist metaphysic. In the "Vorticism"
essay (see *Gaudier-Brzeska*, 84) he wrote: "I said in the preface to my
Guido Cavalcanti that I believed in an absolute rhythm. I believe that every
emotion and every phase of emotion has some toneless phrase, some
rhythm-phrase to express it. . . . To hold a like belief in a sort of permanent metaphor is, as I understand it, 'symbolism' in its profounder sense. It
is not necessarily a belief in a permanent world, but it is a belief in that direction." But this belief "toward" a world of universals does not make him
essentially a Symbolist, any more than his approach to Moderate Realism
makes him essentially a Scholastic philosopher. Though he felt that this
realm was capable of sensible manifestation (through "absolute" metaphor,
or in "magic moments"), his discussion of Images as universals depends on
quite different lines of thought, as I argue in the second section of this
chapter. To repeat: Symbolism is in the background of Imagism but the
one is not a local version of the other. Pound's magical, musical mysticism
(see Chap. Four, esp. the last pages) is a hybrid, not derived from any one
source: we probably ought to stop attributing everything hierophantic in
modern poetry to Symbolist influence.

That he insists on deriving the universals from particulars is nothing against him, and is a belief he must have shared with many great literary artists. W. K. Wimsatt, Jr., observes that "one may see the persistence in literary criticism of a theory that poetry presents the concrete and the universal, or the individual and the universal, or an object which in a mysterious and special way is both highly general and highly particular. The doctrine is implicit in Aristotle's two statements that poetry imitates action and that poetry tends to express the universal." [7] Aristotle had taught that poetry was a higher and more philosophic thing than history: instead of being limited to recording the vagaries of human affairs, what Alcibiades said or did, it may present universal truths in the form of particular events— events not subject to the chances of the world but governed by the laws of consequentiality and design that can be exhibited in a well-made plot. The progeny of this doctrine have been numerous and vastly influential. In the Renaissance, Sidney's claim for poetry was that it surpassed both philosophy and history by combining the best of both, the precept with the example, the universal with the particular. Well before Sidney's time, at least as far back as Boethius, Western thought had begun to entertain Aristotelian solutions for the problem of universals; and some of the occult traditions made "the whole in the part" into a byword. Given new emphases by Hegel and others, the idea takes a new turn in the form of disparaging distinctions between symbolism and "mere" allegory, as Angus Fletcher points out. The keynote is struck by Goethe: "There is a great difference, whether the poet seeks the particular for the general or sees the general in the particular. From the first procedure arises allegory, where the particular serves only as an example of the general; the second procedure, however, is really the nature of

[7] W. K. Wimsatt, Jr., "The Concrete Universal," in *The Verbal Icon: Studies in the Meaning of Poetry* (New York, 1958), 71.

poetry: it expresses something particular, without thinking of the general or pointing to it." The depreciation of allegory is continued by Coleridge:

The Symbolical cannot perhaps be better defined in distinction from the allegorical, than that it is always a part of that, of the whole of which it is representative.—"Here comes a sail,"—(that is a ship) is a symbolical expression. "Behold our lion!" when we speak of some gallant soldier, is allegorical. Of most importance to our present subject is this point, that the latter (allegory) cannot be other than spoken consciously;—whereas in the former (the symbol) it is very possible that the general truth may be unconsciously in the writer's mind during the construction of the symbol.

The importance to Coleridge of this distinction is suggested by the way in which the Imagination/Fancy distinction is embedded in it: allegory is largely the operation of labored, self-conscious Fancy linking "fixities and definites"; symbolism is made by the more powerful and deeper-running force of Imagination, creatively perceiving reality under various aspects and fusing these apprehensions into unities. In another passage Coleridge calls allegory "but a translation of abstract notions into a picture-language. . . . empty echoes which the fancy arbitrarily associates with apparitions of matter." The symbol, on the other hand, "is characterized by a translucence of the special in the individual, or of the general in the special, or of the universal in the general; above all by the translucence of the eternal through and in the temporal. It always partakes of the reality which it renders intelligible; and while it enunciates the whole, abides itself as a living part of that unity of which it is the representative." [8]

The effect of this particular version of the idea on the modern tradition can be observed in the derogatory sense in which the

[8] All quoted from Angus Fletcher, *Allegory: The Theory of a Symbolic Mode* (Ithaca, 1964), 13n, 16–17, 16n.

term "allegory" is now usually employed. Equally modern are the emphases in the statements of Goethe and Coleridge on the peculiar pre-eminence of the real particular; this is a decided change from the earlier emphasis on the universal side of the formula, with the particular only an "example." The change is one from symbol as representation to symbol as synecdoche: Fletcher remarks that "by identifying Symbol with synecdoche, Coleridge is assuming a sort of *participation mystique* of the Symbol with the idea symbolized." [9] As it happens, a more or less permanent part of Pound's poetics was his preference for rigorous synecdochic implication to vague allegorical association in symbolism. The latter method was that of *symboliste* "suggestiveness"; Pound attacked this, and their degrading of symbol to allegory and metonymy, in a passage already quoted (p. 57). For him, "the natural object is always the adequate symbol" of whatever whole it is a part.

That we see the force of a religious belief *(participation mystique)* in the background here must partly explain why the particular was so revered in the whole "Romantic Image" succession, from Blake to the modernists. Separating themselves from Naturalist doctrine, which valued particulars only insofar as they illustrated socio-economic determinisms, the "alienated" artists devoted themselves to the forging of images that blazoned forth literally unspeakable truths in the forms of concrete particulars seized and rendered with a religious intensity. An apotheosis of this tradition is found among the ideas of that priest of the imagination, Joyce, who stated that he chose Dublin to write about "because if I can get to the heart of Dublin I can get to the heart of all the cities of the world. In the particular is contained the universal." [10]

[9] Fletcher, *Allegory,* 17–18. The synecdochic conception is of course essential to the idea of the universal in the particular.

[10] Quoted by William Noon, S.J., in his *Joyce and Aquinas* (New Haven and London, 1957), 60.

The reader is invited to examine the uncanny similarity of
Joyce's little joke to Pound's apprehension of the translucence
of a "universal element" in the local details of Dublin, if he needs
further demonstration that this was the key point in Pound's instinctive understanding of Joyce. The point here is that Joyce's
phrase cannot be dismissed as a mere witticism when put beside
the overwhelming testimony of his work, built out of particulars
in their most aggressively trivial form. Joyce's concern with
trivia did not derive solely from the fact that the word once had
a dignified meaning; he clearly believed that epiphany must
come forth from banality. Richard Ellmann puts it as well as
anyone:

> Other writers had labored tediously to portray it, but no one
> knew what the commonplace really was until Joyce had written.
> There is nothing like Joyce's commonplace in Tolstoy, where
> the characters, however humble, live dramatically and instill
> wisdom or tragedy in each other. Joyce was the first to endow
> an urban man of no importance with heroic consequence. For a
> long time his intention was misunderstood: it was assumed he
> must be writing satire. How else justify so passionate an interest
> in the lower middle class? . . . To look into the flotsam of a city
> was common enough after Zola, but to find Ulysses there was
> reckless and imprudent.

Ellmann concludes that "Joyce's discovery, so humanistic that
he would have been embarrassed to disclose it out of context,
was that the ordinary is the extraordinary." [11] Humanistic that
version may be, but perhaps the Biblical tradition of epiphany

---

[11] *James Joyce*, 3. The further point implied here is that Joyce's use of
Dublin as a particular containing a universal was not only a metaphysical
device, but also a kind of urban variant on the pastoral convention of
Western literature. Since this in turn was largely inspired by the pastoral
metaphors of the Bible, with reference to the tradition that the life of the
Patriarchs was nomadic and shepherdly, we return again to Joyce's religious training for the source of his method. I do not mean to view Joyce,
on the other hand, as merely a "lapsed Catholic"; his attitudes suggest a

out of banality (e.g., theophanies in mangers or on crosses) is more to the point. Joyce's work is hardly orthodox, for Christ and Odysseus become types of Bloom rather than *vice versa,* but it is perhaps the more Biblical for that. His method is a good Catholic one, sacralization of the real particular: the most petty detail may suddenly reveal itself as part of a pattern of reverberating cosmic significance. Where the determinists held that human experience was reducible to significant patterns, Joyce expands it to giant forms. And just because it was unorthodox, Joyce's awareness of the potentially sacramental nature of every scrap of trivia had no theoretical limits; for him there was no necessary subordination to a hierarchy of beings.

Pound makes use of certain similar methods in his own attempt at the re-sacralization of a profaned world, though he is more eclectic in his sources. He can sometimes use the anecdotal in the way Joyce uses the trivial, and he lays a most Catholic stress on the real existence of the particular thing; also like Joyce he is concerned with the details of myth, seeking the moment of metamorphosis which opens into the permanent world of "gods, etc.," as he succinctly puts it.[12] Metamorphosis is a way of showing the true nature of things under the figure of swift and dramatic change; see Ovid, and Dante. Pound's assertions of the truth of myth and the reality of the gods reflect not only the hope of restoring some of the meaning dissipated by reductionist skepticism, but a sense of "striking at universals" through real particulars. These beings are "no abstractions, no figures of

---

revenge on the Church rather than a secular extension of its principles. His hatred of Catholicism was no doubt sincere, as his wife's refusal to let a priest officiate at his funeral testifies (*James Joyce,* p. 755), but he was an indefatigable user of his own past, and was quite capable of seeing meaning in ideas he abominated as beliefs. I cannot persuade myself that the deepest basis of his work is anything other than a kind of theological metaphysic, the fortunate fall into immanence.

[12] *Letters,* 210.

speech" but earthly presences, heavenly truths manifested in apprehensible forms.[13] Imagist poetics reflects a similar pattern: essence is manifested in a real (though usually trivial) event. "Essence" is used here not with a Platonic sense of a transcendent idea of which the particular is only a pale copy, nor with a dualist sense of some pure inner kernel uncorrupted by contact with the material world. Rather the sense is more Aristotelian, stressing potentiality. The best definition is Fenollosa's: "The cherry tree is all that it does." Revelation is through action; an "Image" of a woman is presented by making the scene or event convey the emotion. This last idea, roughly the same as Fenollosa's "objective predication," is like a somewhat demystified version of the Joycean epiphany: the thing itself, the object or action or situation, bursts forth with its own meaning, its own revelation of potentiality. In an Imagist world, things *are* their meanings, and "you cannot distinguish between the thing and its image."

A modern authority says that the purposive structure of the myths of primitive men aims at treating "the sensible properties of the animal and plant kingdoms as if they were the elements of a message," and that their main effort is in "discovering 'signatures.' " [14] Of course the Image (more obviously the ideogram) is a "signature." The conception of reality held by Joyce and Pound recalls the structure, if not the content, of a well-

[13] Pound used the phrases in connection with Dante's visions: see *The Spirit of Romance*, 126. See my discussion in Chap. Four.

[14] Claude Lévi-Strauss, *The Savage Mind* (Chicago, 1966), 268. Lévi-Strauss on myth makes an interesting comparison with Joyce: he says that whereas science discards many things as meaningless, myth tries to make all meaningful, using techniques and materials that are, when judged by the standards of science, makeshift and trivial. "Mythical thought for its part is imprisoned in the events and experiences which it never tires of ordering and re-ordering in its search to find them a meaning. But it also acts as a liberator by its protest against the idea that anything can be meaningless, with which science at first resigned itself to a compromise" (p. 21).

known medieval principle that perhaps descends from the primitive one, that "the whole of nature is, as it were, a hieroglyph of revealed truth; that the strange happenings in Nature's kingdom yield up a kernel of divine teaching. The pelican prefigures Christ and His Charity, the pearl the virgin birth." [15] I am not trying to blur obvious distinctions between the medieval and modern world-views, still less to argue that Pound and Joyce were antiquaries or throwbacks. I assert simply that some of the most powerful ideas of Western Christianity, including that fateful statement of immanence in the doctrine of Incarnation, percolated through various channels and indirect ways until they reached modernism, as it were, devoid of content but intact in shape. Doctrines of Christian immanence, or rather the insight they embody, must be seen in the background of post-Symbolist attempts to repudiate the notion of symbol as mere representation, metaphor as mere analogy or comparison. Northrop Frye takes the trouble to remind us that "the full metaphorical statement 'Christ *is* God and Man' is orthodox, and the Arian and Docetic statements in terms of simile or likeness condemned as heretical." [16] Here the idea of the universal in the particular is raised to its highest power. Here we see why there was nothing *necessarily* irreverent in Lippi's painting a young Florentine wench as the Madonna: since there can be no graven images of things in heaven anyway, your symbol for divinity had better be of the most real and fleshly kind. As for modernism, once the idea of symbol as arbitrary sign was changed to symbol as "living part in that unity of which it is the representative," the way was open to a poetry of reality. To illuminate Imagism May Sinclair turned to the Eucharist which embodies

[15] E. H. Gombrich, *"Icones Symbolicae:* The Visual Image in Neo-Platonic Thought," *Journal of the Warburg and Courtauld Institutes,* XI (1948), 168–69.

[16] Northrop Frye, *Anatomy of Criticism: Four Essays* (Princeton, 1957), 142–43.

the mystic synecdoche of Incarnation: "For them the bread and wine are the body and the blood." To wind up on a properly oracular note, let me quote Norman O. Brown: "Transubstantiation—the whole problem of symbolism. Metaphor is really metamorphosis; and the primal form of the sentence is *Tat tvam assi*, Thou art That; or, of bread and wine, *hoc est corpus meum*, this is my body." [17]

The force of the tradition I am talking about shows in the fact that allegory, at least in its more Alexandrian forms, proved not fully suitable for the interpretation of Scripture and was displaced by typology. Typology insisted on the real historical existence of its symbols, i.e., of its particulars embodying universals, and did not hesitate to relate entities without much surface resemblance: Rahab the harlot was a type of the Church.[18] Not only did this method provide the best way of reading the Old Testament as the foreshadowing of the New, but it reinforced the thrust of Incarnation against analogy and toward symbol as reality. Its norms have had an oblique and disguised effect on our literary norms ever since; as Erich Auerbach tells us, it shaped the Western literary character as *figura;* and on the problem of literary symbolism (the word "type" was used to

[17] Norman O. Brown, *Love's Body* (New York, 1966), 168. For May Sinclair, see "Two Notes," 88–89. Kermode, in *Romantic Image,* 53, comments on Yeats's poem "Michael Robartes and the Dancer": "Robartes' triumphant argument from the Eucharist is, of course, the clinching one; here at any rate the emblem of a thing becomes the thing itself, and a truth of a different order acquires a physical presence, as the Romantic Image must. We are again reminded of Stephen Dedalus, and the Joycean epiphany: 'O! In the virgin womb of the imagination the word was made flesh.' " Joyce of course shared the general hostility to mere simile. Noon *(Joyce and Aquinas,* 63) quotes from a Joyce notebook: "Metaphor prefer to comparison. Comparison makes folks wait and tells you only what something is like."

[18] See Jean Daniélou, S.J., *From Shadows to Reality: Studies in the Biblical Typology of the Fathers,* trans. Dom Wulstan Hibberd (London, 1960), 244 ff. *et passim.* Cf. also Erich Auerbach, "Figura," in *Scenes from the Drama of European Literature* (New York, 1959), and *Mimesis: The Representation of Reality in Western Literature,* trans. Willard Trask (Garden City, N.Y., 1957), esp. pp. 64–66 and 136–41.

mean "symbol" well into the nineteenth century) it suggested that the uniqueness of the real particular, its *haecceitas,* somehow demanded as a complement the idea of eternal sameness in experience. Typology emerges full-blown again in the attitude toward myth of Joyce and Pound, a fact that testifies to their centrality in this tradition of thought. Odysseus sailed the world, Bloom stayed at home, but experience is all the same; Bloom and HCE are identified with a veritable catalogue of figures, and history repeats itself in patterns that turn the real events of life into symbols telling the same story again and again. In our time the closest analogue to this vision is that of the psychiatrist: the patterns of a neurotic's life show how real events can be symbolic and compulsively repetitive. But Joyce would have thought of the older paradigm, the immense tautology of the Christian Church. (St. Augustine says that "Scripture teaches nothing but charity, nor condemns anything but cupidity"; in all its infinite variety the Bible is saying the same thing over and over again, for an orthodox Christian.[19]) When Joyce was framing his version of the one story repeated *ad infinitum* by the whole of Creation, in *Finnegans Wake,* he sought to make it ever more trivial and commonplace on the one hand (as the early sketches show) while extending its symbolic reach to infinity on the other. Part of his technique was an accelerated and compressed typology: characters are constantly becoming each other, and few identities are certain outside the basic fixed relationships. Some have compared the effect to that of a speeded-up movie, but it is more exactly a typology of shadow and *figura* set whirling.

Pound's work too is implicitly typological: not only does Troy crop up in South France, and Actaeon in Vidal, but the themes of "making it new," of survival of mind—in fact the whole metamorphic tradition as Pound uses it—need typological

---

[19] St. Augustine, *On Christian Doctrine,* trans. D. W. Robertson, Jr. (New York, 1958), 88.

interpretation. Even his criticism has a typological conception at its base, for Pound wrote of poetry that it was an art "always the same at root, never the same in appearance for two decades in succession." [20] To sum it all up: one of the deepest assumptions of Pound's poetics is one he shared with Fenollosa and with typology, that the particular is not a "mere pawn" but a body of potentialities capable of revealing itself in surprising ways by being set into certain relationships.

Before it is objected that typology is too remote a source for an American poet, let us remember that America was founded by men for whom England was Egypt, the Atlantic the Red Sea, and New England a Wilderness/Promised Land. Furthermore, as our literary criticism betrays its Biblical and exegetical origins by the moralistic burden it bears, which seems so out of proportion to those of the criticisms of other arts, so the recurrent belief that literature is not fabulistic, so crucial to modernism, revives typology's insistence on the reality of its symbolic material. Typology assumed the historicity of patriarchal narratives—and, interestingly, modern scholarship is looking at this idea with new respect: Pound and his master Frobenius anticipated a general return to the emphasis on the real rather than the fabulistic character of myth, and this return has been a particularly fruitful step for Old Testament research.[21] In

---

20 "Patria Mia, V," *New Age,* XI (1912), 540. Pound probably knew little of Biblical typology, but he was well aware of the similar idea that Rome was a reincarnation of Troy, an idea invented by the Romans but also made much of in the Christian Middle Ages. (See the epigraph to the poem "Rome": "*Troica Roma resurges.*") This belief in turn gave rise to the typological conception of the *translatio,* the movement of power and culture from Troy and Greece to Rome and thence to the West; see Ernst Robert Curtius, *European Literature and the Latin Middle Ages,* Torchbook ed. (New York and Evanston, 1963), 29.

21 William F. Albright's *From the Stone Age to Christianity,* which first appeared in 1940, was one of the important books in the trend toward today's treatments, some learned and some popular, of the Bible "as history."

Joyce and Pound, as we might expect, the idea of the reality of symbols appears in heightened form: for them it has become a fervent thirst for the tang of reality, which they seek to get in their work by what seem at first ridiculously extravagant means. Joyce wrote to his aunt to persuade her to measure the height of the railings at 7 Eccles Street, in order to judge whether Bloom could in fact have jumped over them.[22] Pound admired this kind of obsessive scrupulosity, which he believed to be an almost unnoticeable but vitally important component of lasting literature.

The sheer literary qualities in Homer are such that a physician has written a book to prove that Homer must have been an army doctor. (When he describes certain blows and their effect, the wounds are said to be accurate, and the description fit for coroner's inquest.)

Another French scholar has more or less shown that the geography of the Odyssey is correct geography; not as you would find it if you had a geography book and a map, but as it would be in a "periplum", that is, as a coasting sailor would find it.

The news in the Odyssey is still news.[23]

The examples imply that something more than naturalistic facticity is being appealed to here. The passage contains an uncanny idea, almost a superstition, that literature had better deal accurately with the real world. This was a lesson Pound had learned in his early studies in medieval authors; he remarked of Dante: "His vividness depends much on his comparison by simile to particular phenomena; this we have already noted in the chapter on Arnaut Daniel; thus Dante, following the Provençal, says not 'where a river pools itself,' but 'As at Arles, where the Rhone pools itself.' " [24] Pound pursued this hint far

[22] Ellmann, *James Joyce*, 533.
[23] *ABC of Reading*, 43–44.
[24] *The Spirit of Romance*, 159. Actually Pound had misremembered his own second chapter; see p. 28, where the name of the river is different.

past the method of "comparison by simile." By 1912 he had
erected a standard that called for an accuracy so minute that it
would be visible, as it were, only through a microscope.

An art is vital only so long as it is interpretative, so long, that is,
as it manifests something which the artist perceives at greater
intensity, and more intimately, than his public. If he be the seeing man among the sightless, they will attend him only so long
as his statements seem, or are proven true. . . . The interpretive
function is the highest honor of the arts, and because it is so we
find that a sort of hyper-scientific precision is the touchstone
and assay of the artist's power, of his honor, his authenticity.

.   .   .   .

There is to the artist [in any subject] a like honorable oppor-
tunity for precision, for that precision through which alone can
any of these matters take on their immortality.
    "Magna pars mei," says Horace, speaking of his own futurity,
"that in me which is greatest shall escape dissolution": The *accurate* artist seems to leave not only his greater self, but beside
it, upon the films of his art, some living print of the circum-
volving man. . . . We find these not so much in the words—
which anyone may read—but in the subtle joints of the craft, in
the crannies perceptible only to the craftsman.[25]

What is true of the man in his work must perforce be true of the
work itself: that only through "hyper-scientific precision" can
"any of these matters take on their immortality." Homer sur-
vives because of his accuracy in medicine or geography, or rather because of what they imply about his poem as a whole; Dante
likewise. When Pound defined the epic as "a poem including
history," he may have had in mind more than his thesis that "history that omits economics is mere bunk." [26] He may have meant
that the epic progresses from storehouse for the tribal lore to ve-

25 "Psychology and Troubadours," first published in *The Quest,* IV
(1912); included in editions of *The Spirit of Romance* after 1932, as
Chapter Five; in my edition, pp. 87–88.
26 *Literary Essays,* 86; *Guide to Kulchur,* 259; cf. *Letters,* 247.

hicle for a wider kind of knowledge, "history" in accurate details rather than generalities. In that sense, he wanted the *Cantos*
to be an epic: hence the chunks of documents, correspondence,
etc. He remarked of Joyce's *Ulysses* that "in this super-novel
our author has also poached on the epic." The fanatic zeal of
Joyce and Pound to get the real into their work was for them a
natural development out of literary tradition.[27] It may be that
Papist superstition and the reading of too many naturalist novels
played a part in Joyce's awe of the fact, but the basic cause must
be sought in the ancestry of our literary ideas, and we find it
whether we look to the Bible or to Homer.

Let us turn to a more specific problem of poetics: the issue of
particularization brings up the apparent puzzle of the Imagist
hatred of adjectives. Pound, and Aldington too, frequently made
contemptuous sneers at "painted adjectives" that impede the
"shock and stroke" of the poetry. At first glance this would seem
to run counter to the principle of particularization: are not adjectives commonly used for greater specificity? Is not a "blue
gown" more particular than a "gown"? This is a problem that
Wimsatt, too, has dealt with; he also finds adjectives a problem
in maintaining what he calls "the substantive level." Unfortunately he assumes that "twentieth century imagism" necessitates
lots of adjectives, and ignores the fulminations against them in
Pound's propaganda. But he opens several fruitful lines for in-
quiry: "The general direction of philosophy from Locke to
Kant," he says, leads to the valuation "of qualities over things.
When the proper names and essences of things had been de-
prived of any special dignity, the things themselves easily became less impressive than their definitions, their periphrases,
their qualitative connotations." [28] This trend partly accounts for
the late eighteenth-century development of "poetic diction"

[27] *Literary Essays*, 406.
[28] "The Substantive Level," *Verbal Icon*, 139–41.

composed of adjectival circumlocution and periphrasis; modernism seems bent on going far beyond Romanticism to reverse this trend. The trouble is that poetry following the trend must be largely descriptive and depend almost entirely on adjectives. Pound had harsh things to say about description and explicitly differentiated the presentative method from it; for overmuch qualification of things by adjectives lessens the sense of reality in the particular by placing emphasis on the vague general kinds of secondary qualities. No longer is it the unique and particular gown that matters, but only the kind to which it belongs: "*blue* gown." Such usage only pigeonholes the object instead of truly particularizing.

The same point may be put another way in terms of "presentational immediacy." Excess of adjectives weakens "presentation" by allowing after-the-fact reflection to color the experience. As early as *The Spirit of Romance* Pound warned against "epithets of secondary apparition or afterthought," such as "*sage* Hippotades" or "*forbidden* tree." These do not "stimulate conviction in the actual vision of the poet." Pound also looked down his nose at poetry that "uses the same adjectives to depict either a woman or a sunset." [29] Again Wimsatt makes a relevant stylistic point: he argues that the style that uses many adjectives and the style that uses abstractions or periphrases are both "internal and reflexive modes of description—expressing on the one hand the intricately sensitive, Proustean awareness of experience in detail, and on the other the dreamy abstractness, the suffused vagueness of revery." [30] Which is to say, both styles are useful for subjective and descriptive arts, but useless for an art that presents "objective predication." Hence the Puritanic hatred of decoration expressed in the Imagist proscription of adjectives (often referred to as "ornaments" or "festoons") was perfectly

29 *The Spirit of Romance*, 159; *Literary Essays*, 294.
30 "The Substantive Level," *Verbal Icon*, 144.

suited to the dynamic principle of the poetry. "Direct" and "naked" were terms often used in informed critiques of Imagism, notably that of May Sinclair: if the particular was to contain the universal, it had to be stark and unencumbered, full of a radiant "thisness" of its primary being, not veiled by secondary qualities.

One more point: the fanatic desire of Pound and Joyce to get the real into their works had nothing to do with a desire to abandon language. They do not "obscurely wish that poetry could be written with something other than words," in Kermode's unfortunate phrase.[31] That may apply to Hulme, who wanted intuitions or "sensations handed over bodily," but I think I have sufficiently indicated that Pound's attitude toward language was different from Hulme's. Hulme's true descendant may well be a contemporary disciple of the objectist school, Jack Spicer, who writes in his "Letter to Lorca": "I would like to make poems out of real objects. The lemon to be a lemon that the reader could cut or squeeze or taste—a real lemon like a newspaper in a collage is a real newspaper."[32] Pound and Joyce had more faith in language than that. It is just Pound's faith in language, his Realism, that enabled him to believe that he could get the universal as well as the particular into the Image. To that process we now turn our attention.

IMAGES AS "LORDS OVER FACT": THE SHAPES OF EXPERIENCE

Pound made many statements about particularization, but about universals he was more reticent. Only once did he write an extended discussion of the problem; this is embedded in an

---

[31] *Romantic Image*, 136.

[32] *The New American Poetry: 1945–1960*, 413. I am being a little unfair to Spicer by not quoting the rest of his "letter"; in one sense it is merely an extreme statement of a desire for a "poetry of reality." But there is still a world of difference between his attitude toward language and Pound's.

essay on the relation of Imagism to the plastic arts. The theses of
the essay are helpful preparations for the analysis of Images as
universals. Specifically, in relating Imagism to Vorticism, Pound
explained:

Whistler said somewhere in the *Gentle Art:* "The picture is interesting not because it is Trotty Veg, but because it is an ar-
rangement in colour." The minute you have admitted that, you
let in the jungle, you let in nature and truth and abundance and
cubism and Kandinsky, and the lot of us. Whistler and Kandinsky and some cubists were set to getting extraneous matter
out of their art; they were ousting literary values. The Flau-
bertians talk a good deal about "constatation." "The 'nineties"
saw a movement against rhetoric. I think all these things move
together, though they do not, of course, move in step.[33]

The passage is interesting because of the links it makes between
Whistler's defiant scorn for "pictures that tell a story" and
Pound's contempt for plot, rhetoric and other "literary values."
But it is still more interesting because it suggests that one way to
come at the broader aspects of Imagism might be to consider
some points about images that were brought into focus in those
early days of modern art. A brief summary of these points is
found in a little essay by E. H. Gombrich, called "Meditations on
a Hobby Horse or The Roots of Artistic Form." Gombrich
deals with the question of images as "representational" or "abstract" by beginning with a child making a hobbyhorse out of a
stick. The child has little interest in representing a horse in any
imitative sense, or in abstracting an idea of "horseness" for por-
trayal. "The stick is neither a sign signifying the concept horse
nor is it a portrait of an individual horse. By its capacity to serve
as a 'substitute' the stick becomes a horse in its own right, it belongs in the class of 'gee-gees' and may even merit a proper name
of its own." [34] I assume that Gombrich sets off the term "sub-

[33] The essay was "Vorticism" (see note 11, Chap. One). *Gaudier-
Brzeska*, 85.
[34] Because the whole essay is relevant to my argument, I have assumed

stitute" to make it clear that the hobbyhorse is not a copy of a horse, but, as he emphasizes, a horse "in its own right"; here is a way in which the image becomes in a sense indistinguishable from the thing, the particular from the universal. The image is autonomous even though it would be unimaginable without the existence of real horses, and is not mimetic even though it may have been made as a result of perceptions of real horses. Nor is the hobbyhorse a creature of the familiar "expressive" aesthetic that replaced the mimetic one in the nineteenth century. It is not "expressive" in the sense of an exteriorization of personality, nor even in the sense of a personal message from the artist to the world: "Communication need not come into this process at all. He may not have wanted to show his horse to anyone. It just served as a focus for his fantasies as he galloped along." Nor is the hobbyhorse an autonomous image in the expressionist sense, for it cannot be either purely expressive or purely free and abstract: it must have some relation to horses. By leaving behind the expressionist idea we go on to the twentieth century, and to Imagism.

I have suggested that Imagism desired the essentiality of the conceptual image combined with the definiteness of the perceptual image. Conceptual images, the class to which the hobbyhorse belongs, are given a biological basis by Gombrich, who notes that young birds or fishes can be made to mistake simple dots or round forms for their parents.

An "image" in this biological sense is not an imitation of an object's external form but an imitation of certain privileged or relevant aspects. . . . The artist who goes out to represent the

---

that, as with the Fenollosa essay, the reader who is interested enough to check quotations will want to check the whole thing, so I have omitted individual page citations. See E. H. Gombrich, *Meditations on a Hobby Horse and Other Essays on the Theory of Art* (London and Greenwich, Conn., 1963), 1–11. There is a reprint in Josephine Miles, ed., *Classic Essays in English* (2nd ed.; Boston and Toronto, 1965), 408–22.

visible world is not simply faced with a neutral medley of forms he seeks to "imitate." Ours is a structured universe whose main lines of force are still bent and fashioned by our biological and psychological needs, however much they may be overlaid by cultural influences. We know that there are certain privileged motifs in our world to which we respond almost too easily. The human face may be outstanding among them. Whether by instinct or by very early training, we are certainly ever disposed to single out the expressive features of a face from the chaos of sensations that surrounds it, and to respond to its slightest variations with fear or joy.

It would seem that these "privileged or relevant" motifs could be related to the "complexes" of Imagism, which also assumes a world structured on "objective lines of relations," to use Fenollosa's phrase. Gombrich continues: "At the most primitive level, then, the conceptual image might be identified with what we have called the minimum image—the minimum, that is, which will make it fit into a psychological lock." The two dots that will fool young fishes fit the psychological lock of the response to the mother fish; mere hasty lines resembling even slightly the features of a face can call forth an emotional response from humans because, as Gombrich remarks, this psychological lock is almost too easy to fit. We can see faces in clouds, or patterns on a wall.

As in a few pencil lines we may recognize the image of a face, so the Imagist seeks to present a recognizable "complex" in a few disciplined lines of poetry. Recognition as an analogy for the desired effect is much better than mere vision, since it includes the kind of involuntary creative insight that is as essential to Imagist theory as it is to Coleridge's Imagination. Of course the Imagist does not often use such privileged motifs as that of the face, but he does seek the same kind of fitting of the psychological lock that constitutes recognition. Indeed, the very anecdote that seems to sum up the Imagist "presentative method," that of Flaubert teaching De Maupassant to describe a concierge, shows that recognizability is the best analogue: if you can present the concierge so that the reader could recognize her, you may be sure that you have made an Image of her. The aim of Imagism, as of the child making the hobbyhorse, is to produce in the most economical way an apprehensible, recognizable form. The shape must be reduced to elements having "privileged or relevant aspects." The recognizability is attained by the combination of definiteness and essentiality: the image must present a precisely rendered particular scene or object, yet must be an essence too, since the psychological locks are constructed to open to "universal" keys—the baby bird responds to what would seem to us a very general and abstract image, the barest possible representation of birdness. Imagism's merging of essentiality and definiteness, of conceptual and perceptual images, is in fact the determinative form of the particular containing the universal.

Once aim of Pound's poetics seems to be the construction of a morphology of experience in the form of images. He renders bare, skeletal shapes of insight or feeling, creating in quick strokes the recognizable forms. Ideally the poems have no shape or form except what is produced by the applying of energy to material in the particular poem; hence the poems often seem formless to those accustomed to more traditional kinds. Yet if the poems are indeed quests for universal forms in particular images, their formal aspirations are far more ambitious than those of traditional kinds. Even to contribute to a morphology of experience is a rather high aim. If such was the ultimate goal of Imagism it helps further to explain statements like "It is better to present one Image in a lifetime than to produce voluminous works."

Pound made this aspiration fairly clear in the one extended discussion of Images as universals, which comes near the end of the essay on Imagism and the plastic arts. To make his point he

used a comparison of poems to complicated equations, with the
striking comment that "the difference between art and analyt-
ical geometry is the difference of subject-matter only."

Thus, we learn that the equation $(x-a)^2 + (y-b)^2 = r^2$ governs the circle. It is the circle. It is not a particular circle, it is
any circle and all circles. It is nothing that is not a circle. It is
the circle free of space and time limits. It is the universal. . . . The
statements of "analytics" are "lords" over fact. They are the
thrones and dominations that rule over form and recurrence.
And in like manner are great works of art lords over fact, over
race-long recurrent moods, and over tomorrow.

Pound appended a specific link to Imagism lest his readers miss
the point that "complexes" are supposed to get free of space and
time limits also: "Great works contain this . . . sort of equation.
They cause form to come into being. By the 'image' I mean such
an equation, not an equation of mathematics, not something
about *a*, *b*, and *c*, having something to do with form, but about
sea, cliffs, night, having something to do with mood." [35] Occasionally in prior writings Pound had stated that poetry gives
"equations for emotions," and earlier in this very article he had
made the puzzling assertion that the "symbolist *symbols* have a
fixed value, like numbers in arithmetic, like 1, 2, and 7. The
imagiste's images have a variable significance, like the signs *a*, *b*,
and *x* in algebra." Until he explained how equations signified
universals of experience, these comments were unclear. But the
explanation makes equations seem quite good analogues of what
Pound had in mind for Imagism. Equations are precise and definite, and undeniably register universal "shapes of experience."
Once you learn to read them, you can recognize without hesi-
tation the forms they express. In praising the "qualities of vivid
presentation" in the Chinese original of "The Jewel Stairs'

[35] *Gaudier-Brzeska*, 91–92. Cf. "The Wisdom of Poetry," *The Forum*,
XLVII (1912), 497–501, especially 500.

Grievance" (see page 32), Pound commented: "Upon careful examination we find that everything is there, not merely by 'suggestion' but by a sort of mathematical process of reduction." [36] In short, this terse, skeletal poem is an equation for an emotion.

An equation in this sense is a transposable registration of definite relationships. Pound's assumption is that significant experience comes to us in such shapes, an assumption reminiscent of some of those of Gestalt psychology. Wolfgang Köhler, fighting against Behaviorism and the simpleminded stimulus-response formula of "machine theory," insisted that experience comes to us in patterns of configurations, "segregated wholes," rather than in isolated bits: "Gestalt Psychology claims that it is precisely the original segregation of circumscribed wholes which makes it possible for the sensory world to appear so utterly imbued with meaning to the adult; for, in its gradual entrance into the sensory field, meaning follows the lines drawn by natural organization; it usually enters into segregated wholes." In this conception the transposability of certain patterns is crucial, and Köhler drew some of his most telling evidence from experiments demonstrating transposition in visual responses: "Apparently, Lashley has been the first to show that animals 'transpose.' Having been trained to choose, say, the darker of two gray objects, they shift their response when two other objects of the same class are presented. In other words, they choose the object which represents the dark side of the new pair, even if its particular gray has never been presented during the original learning." In short, they respond not to an isolated "stimulus," nor to a series of fragmentary sensations, but to a configuration of relationships which is apprehended all at once.

Since Ehrenfels wanted to show that shape can never be explained in terms of sensations, he laid great stress upon the in-

[36] "Chinese Poetry," *To-day*, III (1918), 55.

variance of visual shape when the brightness, hue, size, and lo-
cation of an object are changed. . . . In this respect, forms in
time behave just like shapes in space: a melody, for instance,
may be given in different keys, and yet remain the same *qua*
melody. Ehrenfels was entirely right when he said that in this
fashion shape and temporal form are clearly established as phenomena *sui generis*.[37]

The recognition of persisting and transposable shapes and forms
was no less vital to the study of images in modern art than it was
to this important trend in modern psychology. Gombrich, ob-
serving that "all art is 'image-making,' " points out that a "conventional vocabulary of basic forms is still indispensable to the
artist":

> Even the artist of an "illusionist" persuasion must make the man-
> made, the "conceptual" image of convention his starting point.
> Strange as it may seem he cannot simply "imitate an object's
> external form" without having first learned how to construct
> such a form. If it were otherwise there would be no need for
> the innumerable books on "how to draw the human figure" or
> "how to draw ships." Wölfflin once remarked that all pictures
> owe more to other pictures than they do to nature. . . . Con-
> trary to the hopeful belief of many artists, the "innocent eye"
> which should see the world afresh would not see it at all. It
> would smart under the painful impact of a chaotic medley of
> forms and colours.

The structuring, in the creation of transposable forms or images,
must proceed by means of relationship. Of course this is true in
many fields: in music the essential fact to be grasped is that the
interval, not the note, is the "atomic particle." Emphasis on relationship, as I have suggested, ought to shoulder some of the burden usually placed on particulars in analyses of Pound's "ideogrammic" method, and it is even more helpful in thinking about

---

[37] Wolfgang Köhler, *Gestalt Psychology*, Mentor ed. (New York, 1959),
82, 117–18.

configurations as "universals." As Köhler put it, "certain conditions must be kept constant if transposing is to be what the term implies. Relations among the stimuli involved must remain approximately the same when the stimuli themselves are changed." [38] Very likely Köhler would have found Fenollosa's dictum that "relations are more real and more important than the things which they relate" a most interesting assertion.

Simple and obvious examples of meaning occurring in configurations rather than bits could be taken from the field of language. In discourse we respond not to isolated words but to patterns of them; sometimes it appears that we can get the drift of a discourse even when we cannot distinguish the individual words, as in a conversation heard through a wall, whereas if someone speaks French to me (such is my French) I can get a good number of the words but miss the drift because I cannot perceive the patterns. Köhler pointed out that even many "isolated" words are, as it were, dead synecdoches: "The same reference to larger wholes is implied in many terms which we continually use as banal words. We do not generally realize that the meaning of such words points beyond the local facts to which the words may seem to be attached. . . . In the case of thought processes an event is a 'disturbance' only with regard to a larger and otherwise unitary whole which it interrupts." [39] Köhler's other examples were taken from the large number of general words that once had specific spatial or motional meanings, but the list could be extended. If language is as full of dead synecdoche as it is of dead metaphor, then the possibilities for a poetics like Pound's are wide indeed. Let us recall Pound's comment that in "The Jewel Stairs' Grievance" the implications are made not by " 'suggestion' but by a sort of mathematical process of reduction": that is, the poem is constructed out of synecdochic pos-

[38] *Ibid.*, 118.
[39] *Ibid.*, 121.

sibilities that "implicate" a whole story. Bits of the poem by themselves indicate practically nothing—the steps are wet, her stockings are wet, the moon is out. The tryst, the poignancy, her sensitivity and his lack of it—these are found in the relationship of the elements, which by itself creates the whole.

The interests of a "poetry of reality" would at first seem not very well served by this side of Imagism, for Pound's stress on configuration together with his search for the exact word and the "luminous detail" gives some of the poems the spareness of the equations to which he likened them. Imagist poems lack the kind of "stuff" found in abundance in his earlier work. The structuring, formalizing tendency, the desire to delineate the shapes of experience, makes it impossible for Pound to spend time on a leisurely accretion of the kind of detail that yields what we commonly call realism. We know that Pound never cared for poetry that was scenic ("viewy") or realistic in a representational way: one can see a better "picture" in a poem by, say, Amy Lowell. As I have remarked, Pound's Imagism was visual only to the end of precisely presenting complex relationships in process; similarly, it is substantive only to the end of achieving that relation to reality necessary for objective predication. It could not pause to "set the scene" with lots of little realistic touches. We have already noted, in Chapter One, that Pound was concerned to improve on Hueffer's technique on just this point of eliminating the superfluous detail with which an Impressionist "prepares effects." But the "directness" and "nakedness" of bare outlines can give a realism of a different kind. We get in the Imagist period poems like this:

PAGANI'S, NOVEMBER 8

Suddenly discovering in the eyes of the very beautiful
        Normande cocotte
The eyes of the very learned British Museum assistant.

Pagani's was no doubt a real place, and the experience was doubtless real too; the British Museum assistant was probably Laurence Binyon, though I can't furnish the lady's name. Yet the effect of reality is achieved not by the multiplication of such details, but by the swift delineation of a very subtle and evanescent experience. As we might expect, Pound is more interested in apprehending the shape of the experience than in giving it "stuff." Here is an illustration of the structuring tendency without particular references:

THE ENCOUNTER

All the while they were talking the new morality
Her eyes explored me.
And when I arose to go
Her fingers were like the tissue
Of a Japanese paper napkin.

Pound is here so interested in fidelity to the shape of the experience that he has not only stripped it of inessential detail but even of the expectable "punch line." On this poem George T. Wright comments: "Here the effect is of the fragility and delicacy of the thing said. If the last line comprises a resolution, it is not a resolution of discursive or narrative suspense, but of an incomplete abstract (and humorous) design, like an unresolved musical chord." In fact, quite a few of Pound's poems seem like jokes with unclear punch lines—they forego "point" as the *Cantos* forego "plot," for these are "literary values" rather than experiential ones and must be "ousted." Wright observes that "Pound's poetry rests on his rejection of formal rhetorical patterns as the basis of poetic structure. In almost all English poetry an argument leads to a climax; English poets arrange with infinite variety a sequence of climactic sections .... in such a way as to emphasize their discursive continuity, to build up toward a cli-

max, to bring home each point with a bang." [40] He might have
added that Pound's desire to represent the forms of experience
causes him to abandon this rhetorical pattern together with the
traditional poetic forms in which it is usually expressed; in the
poem above this desire causes him to reduce the experience to
details that reveal the main "lines of force" in the moment of the
leave-taking. In such poems, there is no attempt to build up the
scene, but instead an attempt to cut it down to absolute essen-
tials, almost to Gombrich's "minimum" image.

The consequence of this Imagist discipline can be illustrated
by comparison of an Imagist poem with a pre-Imagist one that
has obvious similarities and useful differences. First the pre-
Imagist poem:

BALLATETTA

The light became her grace and dwelt among
Blind eyes and shadows that are formed as men;
Lo, how the light doth melt us into song:

The broken sunlight for a healm she beareth
Who hath my heart in jurisdiction.
In wild-wood never fawn nor fallow fareth
So silent light; no gossamer is spun
So delicate as she is, when the sun
Drives the clear emeralds from the bended grasses
Lest they should parch too swiftly, where she passes.

The poem attempts an evocation of airy lightness, but the comparative lushness of evocative effects, together with the somewhat pretentious diction, makes it feel rather heavy-laden. And
it is much vaguer than the Imagist poem, a study in severe delineation:

[40] George T. Wright, *The Poet in the Poem: The Personae of Eliot,
Yeats, and Pound* (Berkeley and Los Angeles, 1960), 125–26.

GENTILDONNA

She passed and left no quiver in the veins, who now
Moving among the trees, and clinging
                    in the air she severed,
Fanning the grass she walked on then, endures:
Grey olive leaves beneath a rain-cold sky.

The Imagist poem seems more real and yet depends less on
"stuff" or matter; its terseness skeletalizes the moment to an essentiality. The early poem is a pleasant fiction, delicate but con-
trived; the later one presents the irreducible traces of vivid experience. Thus, in the end, the Imagist poem is nearer to a
"poetry of reality" precisely because its main effort went into
structure rather than material. In Pound's words, it is a "lord
over fact," as the earlier one could never be. "Gentildonna" is
indeed an adequate illustration of why the Imagist discipline
produces the universal *in* the particular, for it is a particular
experience universalized without being generalized. This is
exactly the distinction that Gombrich makes in explaining the
inadequacy of the eighteenth-century idea that an artist, to
represent a universal, "disregards the particular and 'generalizes
the forms.'" He uses Madame Tussaud's wax effigies to refute
Sir Joshua Reynolds' assertion that a particular man is merely
"a defective model": "Those in the galleries which are labelled
are 'portraits of the great.' The figure on the staircase made to
hoax the visitor simply represents 'an' attendant, one member of
a class. It stands there as a 'substitute' for the expected guard—
but it is not more 'generalized' in Reynolds' sense." Once again
Gombrich has given us the perfect example, for the wax guard
not only illustrates the universal in the particular, but also, more
slily, May Sinclair's challenge: "You cannot distinguish between
the thing and its image." Many visitors to Madame Tussaud's
must have felt just that way.

"Gentildonna" compared to "Ballatetta" illustrates what Pound would have called the superiority of "the hard" over "the soft." After Imagism Pound practiced "the hard" with such dedication that his highest praise for a poem came out in terms of "hard light and clear edges." Helping Eliot to revise the manuscript of the *Waste Land*, Pound deprecated his own work by comparison: "Complimenti, you bitch. I am wracked by the seven jealousies, and cogitating an excuse for always exuding my deformative secretions in my own stuff, and never getting an outline. I go into nacre and objets d'art." [41] But dissatisfaction with his achievement did not prevent Pound from continuing to seek the mastery of outline that would yield "shapes of experience." The great majority of the post-1912 poems, even those least obviously "Imagist," show this structuring, skeletalizing, outlining tendency: no matter whether they are erotic, didactic, witty, or bitter, they all try to present a precise configuration of the insight or feeling. Pound's critical vocabulary tells the same story; it became dominated by "hardness," "hard-edgedness," "cutting in hard stone," and other terms suggestive of carving a clear definite outline. He grew obsessed with sculptural metaphors, and suggested that the art of poetry "is as simple as the sculptor's direction: 'Take a chisel and cut away all the stone you don't want.' " [42] To cut the precise outline meant getting rid of distracting mass or "stuff"; it meant getting down to a few "luminous details" to which the psychological locks would open.

I have argued elsewhere how important for Pound was "exact definition," in every sense, and George Dekker has even suggested that a sense of precisely defined boundaries and outlines underlies Pound's use of terms like "character" and "modera-

[41] *Letters*, 38 and 169.
[42] *Ibid.*, 91.

tion." [43] "With usura the line grows thick": the exactness of the suave bounding-line which Pound seeks is needful in that kind of art concerned with registering "immaterial relations" in fields of force; in a heavier mode solidities fix themselves with their own massiness, and do not require clear delimitation. Botticelli, not Rubens, is Pound's ideal painter.

> all that Sandro knew, and Jacopo
>   and that Velásquez never suspected
> lost in the brown meat of Rembrandt
>   and the raw meat of Rubens and Jordaens
>   (Canto LXXX)

Judging from the number of poems that present it, one of Pound's favorite kinds of "immaterial relations" that required this kind of severe outlining involves the invisible currents of energy that are created when men and women pass close to each other. Pound apprehends sex as a kind of magnetic field, almost literally—in contrast to Mauberley, whose insensitivity to these forces is a sign of his downfall. In Pound's poems we miss the weight of flesh on flesh, but feel the force of pressures and attractions, as in "Tame Cat": "The purring of the invisible antennae/ Is both stimulating and delightful." Here was a fair field indeed for the registration of "shapes of experience."

Sex by no means exhausts the topics presented in the post-Imagist poetry, of course, but it epitomizes the method because it lays an automatic stress on the invisible pressures and edges of experience: in a sexual encounter the "lines of force" dramatize themselves and can easily be implicated in a few details. Yet we must read these poems very closely: because of their reti-

---

[43] My argument is in "Vorticism and the Career of Ezra Pound," *Modern Philology*, LXV (1968), 214–27. See George Dekker, *Sailing After Knowledge: The Cantos of Ezra Pound* (London, 1963), 6–7.

cence, bareness and synecdochic implication they give an appearance of being narrow in emotional scope, and thin in depth. That judgment probably will be modified by any attempt to grasp all that the poems try to do. Images as universals—configurations, equations, transposable shapes—must be read, because of their severe discipline no less than their synecdochic aspirations, as the tips of icebergs. Sometimes the cold appearance may put us off, but it is certain that we cannot begin to comprehend them unless we try to imagine what is implied beneath the surface projections.

Joyce had the advantage over Pound in that he could make use of the novelistic accretion of detail, and thus his work seems more "realistic" than Pound's. But the underlying assumptions of both included a sense of potentiality in the particular, and a sense of the configurational, relational character of experience, and from these assumptions proceeded not only the use of synecdoche as the method of their symbolism, but also a generally organicist world-view—each part of the world ultimately related to every other part—that permitted the further developments of their arts. An Imagist world is precisely the opposite of what Graham Hough sees it as: "A world composed of atomic notations, each image separate from all the others." [44] Only an organicist view, at least in modern times, allows for the possibilities of *universalia in rebus*. An organicist philosopher like Whitehead might have made a good critic of this side of modernism; at any rate, these assumptions bespeak the basic character of thought in the early twentieth century, and Pound and Joyce are no less typical of their age than Whitehead, or Köhler. Modernism's typical goal, from almost any starting

[44] Hough, *Image and Experience: Studies in a Literary Revolution*, 13. See Alfred North Whitehead, *Process and Reality: An Essay in Cosmology*, Torchbook ed. (New York, 1960), 76: "Every so-called 'particular' is universal in the sense of entering into the constitutions of other actual entities."

point, is a poetry of reality, and the belief in universals-in-particulars is eminently fitted for striving toward that end. William Carlos Williams tells us about the "local," and that we should have "no ideas but in things": it is tempting to suspect that Pound's essays on Joyce and Eliot struck the metaphysical chords in him, in spite of his mistrust of "internationalism." In the end they all turned out to be going the same journey.

FOUR

TRADITION, MYTH,
AND IMAGIST POETICS

THE QUEST of modernism for sanctions from the past
needs more examination. The modernists toyed occasionally with such nihilistic nonsense as Futurism and Dadaism,
but these would not support a genuine intellectual structure, so
they turned to the construction of doctrines of tradition that
would validate their various endeavors. The modernist habit is
to defend the most innovative experiments with precedents not
only traditional but sometimes primitivistic. This had been a
tactic employed for centuries, but modernism displays more
than usual anxiety about its foundations. At the same time it was
marked by a need to get free of the past, of its *mortmain*. As
Pound said in 1914, "We are all futurists to the extent of believing with Guillaume Appollonaire [*sic*] that 'On ne peut pas
porter *partout* avec soi le cadavre de son père.' " [1] But he was
sure that a revolutionary step toward freedom would move in
the direction of recovering true tradition, not away from it.

The reactions and "movements" of literature are scarcely, if
ever, movements against good work or good custom. Dryden

[1] *Gaudier-Brzeska*, 82.

and the precursors of Dryden did not react against *Hamlet*. . . . only the mediocrity of a given time can drive the more intelligent men of that time to "break with tradition."

I take it that the phrase "break with tradition" is currently used to mean "desert the more obvious imbecilities of one's immediate elders"; at least, it has had that meaning in the periodical mouth for some years. Only the careful and critical mind will seek to know how much tradition inhered in the immediate elders.[2]

The classic modern statement of the need for tradition is found in T. S. Eliot's essay of 1919, "Tradition and the Individual Talent." From time to time it has been suspected that Pound had something to do with that essay's ideas, a suspicion enhanced by certain parallels between Eliot's doctrines and theses that Pound had been proclaiming for several years. What matters here is not influence or the paternity of ideas, but how the "tradition" on which Pound spent so much effort integrated itself into his poetics and poetry. We know that much of Pound's prose in the twenties and thirties preached a doctrine of salvation through worship of the "inventors and masters" of the art of poetry. What is the relationship of that doctrine, and Eliot's, to the *Cantos?* General assertions about this relationship are often made, but it still needs much illumination.

There were several stages in Pound's thinking on tradition. Adolescent fascination with the very idea of "an art" of poetry developed into a zeal for scholarship on favorite texts; he produced an equivalent for a Ph.D. thesis in *The Spirit of Romance*. Although he was dismissed from his first teaching job, academic ambitions were still very much on Pound's mind when he went to London, and in the first years much of his time was spent in study. But friendships in London, especially with some of Yeats's acquaintances, soon led to decidedly unacademic insights

---

[2] "Notes on Elizabethan Classicists," first appearing in the *Egoist*, IV (1917); see *Literary Essays*, 227.

about the nature of "the tradition," particularly about the medieval poets who were Pound's favorites. Medievalism took on a more esoteric meaning, and Pound began the speculations that find expression in the "Medievalism" essay on Cavalcanti, and throughout the *Cantos*. Meanwhile Hueffer's "modernity" showed him the way to Imagism, and forced him out of derivative poetic techniques; for a short while Pound kept the modernist and antiquarian sides of himself separate, but soon began to use Hueffer's insights to make his tradition a usable past. At this point he started prescribing "tradition," first as a corrective for poetic laxness and then as a gospel for the redemption of culture. While promulgating the idea—by himself, with the Vorticists, and with Eliot—he learned to broaden it a great deal: Eliot for instance seems to have taught him respect for areas of the art he had earlier ignored.

The analysis should begin with the precocious student of languages and literatures, whose ambitions are best described by himself. "I knew at fifteen pretty much what I wanted to do. I believed that the 'Impulse' is with the gods; that technique is a man's own responsibility. . . . It is his own fault if he does not become a good artist—even a flawless artist. I resolved that at thirty I would know more about poetry than any man living." [3] He made this confession at twenty-eight, having in mind a sense that London was facilitating the fulfillment of this ambition as graduate school had been unable to do. Writing home from London, he maintained to his parents that he would soon resume academic life, and talked as if he were on an extended *Wanderjahr*. The letters are full of jobs and fellowships he hoped to get, names such as Princeton and Hobart, and they make much of activities like the courses of lectures he gave at the Regent Street

---

[3] "How I Began," *T. P.'s Weekly* (June 6, 1913), 707; reproduced in Stock (ed.) *Ezra Pound: Perspectives*, 1.

Polytechnic in 1908–1909 and 1909–1910. [4] If Pound is "patent-ly a frustrated teacher," it would be only just to recognize that he prepared assiduously for that career. As late as 1914 he was issuing Utopian schemes for a "College of Arts" (with a Vorti-cist faculty), with a prospectus that included an academic justi-fication of his journey to London: "We draw the attention of new students to the fact that no course of study is complete with-out one or more years in London. Scholarly research is often but wasted time if it has not been first arranged and oriented in the British Museum." [5]

London was a super-graduate school not only because of the writers who were there or the resources of the British Museum. Pound found something else:

Besides knowing living artists I have come in touch with the tradition of the dead. I have had in this the same sort of plea-sure that a schoolboy has in hearing of the star plays of former athletes. . . . There is more, however, in this sort of Apostolic Succession than a ludicrous anecdote, for people whose minds have been enriched by contact with men of genius retain the effects of it.
I have enjoyed meeting Victorians and Pre-Raphaelites and men of the nineties through their friends. [6]

He seems to have literally believed in a laying-on of hands: those who had touched the great dead could pass on a power to him. Even such figures as Yeats and Hueffer were valued at first mostly for their mediumship. The trip to London was a *Nekuia*, a journey to the land of the dead, for the young Pound. Wynd-ham Lewis had in mind the Pound of this period when he re-marked that "he has never loved anything living as he has loved

---

[4] The letters are in the American Literature Collection of the Yale University Library. For the syllabus of the lectures, see Norman, *Ezra Pound*, 31–34.
[5] *Letters*, 41.
[6] "How I Began," 707.

the dead." [7] Too young to discriminate among his enthusiasms, Pound reveled in vicarious satisfactions of his desires to know the great masters.

But, as Pound claimed, there was more to these activities than schoolboyish hero-worship. The adolescent awe of "the tradition of the dead" he erected into a conception articulated in *The Spirit of Romance*, oddly reminiscent of Eliot's later proposal that "the whole of the literature of Europe . . . has a simultaneous existence and composes a simultaneous order":

All ages are contemporaneous . . . . This is especially true of literature, where the real time is independent of the apparent, and where many dead men are our grandchildren's contemporaries, while many of our contemporaries have been already gathered into Abraham's bosom, or some more fitting receptacle.
What we need is a literary scholarship, which will weigh Theocritus and Yeats with one balance.[8]

Throughout all of Pound's growth and development thereafter, this goal remained fixed. Between 1910 and 1915 Pound's poetics changed markedly, but in an article of 1915 he listed his own contribution to the thought of the decade as "an active sense not merely of comparative literature, but of the need for a uniform criticism of excellence based on world-poetry, and not of the fashion of any one particular decade of English verse, or even on English verse as a whole. The qualitative analysis in literature (practised but never formulated by Gaston Paris, Reinach in his Manual of Classical Philology, etc.). The Image." [9] Just as the choice of the word "scholarship" rather than "criticism" to "weigh Theocritus and Yeats with one balance" reveals the set

[7] Wyndham Lewis, *Time and Western Man* (New York, 1928), 71.
[8] *The Spirit of Romance*, 8. Note that this preceded Eliot's essay by nine years. I am grateful to A. Walton Litz for pointing out this similarity.
[9] "Analysis of this Decade," *New Age*, XVI (1915), 410; see *Gaudier-Brzeska*, 115.

of his mind, so here do the names of Paris and Reinach to emblematize "the qualitative analysis in literature." Years later Pound said that he wrote the *ABC of Reading* "to follow the tradition of Gaston Paris and S. Reinach," and throughout his writings occur the names of other scholarly heroes like W. P. Ker, J. W. Mackail, Emil Lévy, and even his teachers at Pennsylvania: Felix Schelling, Hugo Rennert, and Cornelius Weygandt.[10] In these formative years Pound saw himself as the inheritor of nineteenth-century scholarship. He was sure that a professorial knowledge was a necessary component of building a proper tradition: "In most countries the only people who know enough of literature to appreciate—i.e. to determine the value of—new productions are professors and students, who confine their attention to the old." [11] He lamented the professorial attitude, but not the equipment.

Evidently Pound envisioned himself as the scholar-poet, whose technique would be founded on a thorough knowledge of tradition garnered by research and investigation of all the possibilities. " 'Thinking that alone worthy wherein the whole art is employed,' " he quoted approvingly from Dante, "I think the artist should master all known forms and systems of metric." [12] Weygandt, one of Pound's teachers, caught an illuminating point about these ambitions. He observed that "Eliot owes as much to Pound almost as he does, self-confessedly, to Arthur Symons, who revealed the French Symbolists to him. The practice of Eliot's verse harks back to Browning, in its jumbling together of various arts and conditions of life. It would seem that the theory that scholarship should underlie creative writing

---

[10] *ABC of Reading*, 11. See *Literary Essays*, 92, 115, 195, 367; *Letters*, 52; and Canto XX.

[11] "Irony, Laforgue, and Some Satire," *Poetry*, XI (1917), 93; see *Literary Essays*, 280.

[12] "Prolegomena" (see note 5, Chap. One); *Literary Essays*, 9.

comes also from Browning, by way of Pound." [13] Weygandt
may well have known from what his student let drop what we
might have suspected anyway, that Browning was in the background of the desire to master scholarship as a base for poetry.
And though Eliot read Browning before he met Pound, Weygandt may also have been right about Pound's ambitions shaping
and reinforcing Eliot's; it is interesting to wonder if the acade-
micism of Eliot's early poetry and criticism would have been
different if his "cher maître" had not had those youthful desires.

The scholar-poet ambition was not a pose; Pound really believed in the interpenetration of art and scholarship. His studies
paved the way for Imagism, for Pound might never have overcome his initial aversion to Hueffer's ideas if he had not discovered for himself the value of "exact definition" and precise
presentation in Dante and his other favorites. Furthermore, it was
in scholarship itself that Pound first saw the possibilities of what
he called "Luminous Detail." This principle he explained in an
article on scholarly method; he asserted that it was basic to all
good scholarship but was being forgotten because of a growing
tendency toward the antithetical method of "multitudinous
detail": "If a man owned mines in South Africa he would know
that his labourers dug up a good deal of mud and an occasional
jewel, looking rather like the mud about it. If he shipped all the
mud and uncut stones northward and dumped them in one heap
on the shore of Iceland, in some inaccessible spot, we should not
consider him commercially sound. In my own department of
scholarship I should say the operations are rather of this com-
plexion." What was needed, according to Pound, was a scrutiny
bent on the kind of facts that "govern knowledge as the switchboard governs an electric circuit," that offer something he later
called "direct knowledge": "Any fact is, in a sense, 'significant.'

[13] Cornelius Weygandt, *The Time of Yeats: English Poetry of To-day
Against an American Background* (New York and London, 1937), 11.

Any fact may be 'symptomatic,' but certain facts give one a sudden insight into circumjacent conditions, into their causes, their effects, into sequence, and law." Here we have, a few months before the creation of Imagism, a preview of "presentative" method. Pound saw nothing odd in proposing that his critique of scholarship should be applied to poetry. He complained that the same tendency toward "multitudinous detail" that deadened scholarship was creeping into literature: "As scholarship has erred in presenting all detail as if of equal import, so also in literature, in a present school of writing we see a similar tendency." The correct method, on the other hand, had one severe rule: "The artist seeks out the luminous detail and presents it. He does not comment. His work remains the permanent basis of psychology and metaphysics." [14] Perhaps this is where Pound began to use the term "present" in his special sense; the stress on the detail embodying the insight, together with the prohibition on comment, certainly suggests this. Moreover, the Image free of time and space limits is forecast by the identification of the artist's work as the "permanent basis of psychology and metaphysics," and that last word implies a fateful belief that prepared Pound for the Joycean lesson that great art consisted of the universal in the particular—here, the permanence in the detail.

The kind of knowledge transmitted in the "Luminous Detail," as opposed to the merely symptomatic one, played a part in Pound's development of his idea of tradition into a canon of important authors: the writers to study, the members of the true tradition, he identified as those who somehow furnish such insights. In *How to Read*, the emphasized distinction is between those who actually add something timeless to the art of writing, and the "men who do more or less good work in the more or less good style of a period," like Virgil and Petrarch. But the myste-

14 "A Rather Dull Introduction," 130–31.

rious "direct knowledge" figures more openly in an earlier version of the distinction:

> Interesting works are of two sorts, the "symptomatic" and the "donative" . . . in [the first] we find a reflection of tendencies and modes of a time. They mirror obvious and apparent thought movements. They are what one might have expected in such and such a year and place. They register.
> But the "donative" author seems to draw down into the art something which was not in the art of his predecessors. If he also draw from the air about him, he draws latent forces or things present but unnoticed, or things perhaps taken for granted but never examined.[15]

This passage in turn reflects Pound's early belief that "the best of knowledge is 'in the air,' or if not the best, at least the leaven." [16] The knowledge of an era is hidden in innocuous-looking details which give up their significance only when "presented" in contexts structured to bring out their latencies. This thought is commonplace enough, but Pound's faith in these Luminous Details goes almost to the level of mysticism. Hints of his belief are found in certain loosely Bergsonian metaphors in his writings ("Art is a fluid moving above or over the minds of men" or "a river") that express his sense that "the tradition" is at least potentially ever-present, and that there exists a world of these particulars of knowledge, which makes available to us forgotten truths from past centuries embedded in the works of the artists of the time.[17]

The tinge of mysticism in Pound's conception seems to have had something to do with certain people he met in London, notably G. R. S. Mead and Allen Upward. Both knew Yeats, and Pound very likely met them in the circle of esoteric thinkers who frequented Yeats's "Mondays" in London. Upward had

---

[15] Pound, "A Beginning," *New Age*, X (1911), 179.
[16] "A Rather Dull Introduction," 130.
[17] *The Spirit of Romance*, 7.

briefly dabbled with Yeats in psychic experiments, and was in those years correlating spiritualist doctrines with primitive magic-lore in an attempt to demonstrate that all religious phenomena, including Christianity, were results of "some power still working to mould our planetary fates." Upward conceived this power to be "more complex but not less trustworthy than the law of gravitation"; he gave as a reason for believing in such forces the example of electricity, "only the most coarse and obvious of the ethereal . . . influences forever at work weaving the woof of Life upon the warp of Matter." [18] Pound repeatedly proclaimed Upward's works "as interesting philosophically as any that have been written in our time," and prophesied that "what Mr. Upward says will be believed in another twenty or fifty or a hundred years"; he called Upward's mind "as clear as Bacon's," and said that "his middles are less indefinite than Plato's." Even years later he remarked with some pride: "I suppose I am sole reader of all Upward's books, now surviving." Pound was apparently first attracted to the books by their utility for his Romance studies; reviewing Upward's *Divine Mystery* he mentioned this: "I, personally, find in it clues and suggestions for the Provençal love customs of the Middle Ages." [19] This was so, too, with Mead, a well-known figure in occult circles. Pound wrote to his parents high praise of some lectures by Mead that he attended in December, 1911, and shortly thereafter he contributed to Mead's journal of religious arcana, *The Quest*, an article on Provençal sexual mysticism called "Psychology and Troubadours." In it he noted that "a recent lecture by Mr. Mead

[18] Allen Upward, *The Divine Mystery: A Reading of the History of Christianity Down to the Time of Christ* (Boston and New York, 1915). The English edition of this work appeared in 1913, according to Pound (*Letters*, 25). For Upward's connection with Yeats, see his anonymous *Some Personalities* (London, 1921), 57–58.

[19] "Allen Upward Serious," *New Age*, XIV (1914), 779; *Letters*, 296; review of the *Divine Mystery* in *New Freewoman*, I (1913), 207.

on Simon Magus has opened my mind to a number of new possibilities. There would seem to be in the legend of Simon Magus
and Helen of Tyre a clearer prototype of 'chivalric love' than in
anything hereinafter discussed. I recognize that all this matter
of mine may have to be reconstructed or at least re-oriented
about that tradition." [20]

Though he disclaimed immediate influence from Mead, the
article shows that he had been toying with some fairly esoteric
ideas. Picking up hints from Joséphin Péladan's *Le Secret des
troubadours,* Pound proceeded to ask:

Did this "close ring," this aristocracy of emotion, evolve, out of
its half memories of Hellenistic mysteries, a cult—a cult stricter,
or more subtle, than that of the celibate ascetics, a cult for the
purgation of the soul by a refinement of, and lordship over, the
senses?

.   .   .   .

Did this "chivalric love," this exotic, take on mediumistic properties? Stimulated by the color or quality of emotion, did that
"color" take on forms interpretive of the divine order? Did it
lead to an "exteriorization of the sensibility," and interpretation
of the cosmos by feeling? [21]

These speculations were based on two assumptions: one, that
sex can have a double purpose, "reproductive and educational;
or, as we see in the realm of fluid force, one sort of vibration
produces at different intensities, heat and light." This statement suggests that the light that so often occurs in Pound's
poetry in connection with creativity is of distinctly erotic con-

[20] See note 25, Chap. Three; *The Spirit of Romance,* 91. The letters are
in the Yale Collection.
[21] *The Spirit of Romance,* 90 and 94. Students of medieval literature will
recognize Pound's use of the standard hypotheses about "courtly love" in
these pages, an indication of how much Pound read Gaston Paris and his
followers. Pound makes heavy use, naturally, of the "pagan survival" explanation.

figuration.[22] With the help of Remy de Gourmont's *Physique de l'amour*, Pound carried the idea further; in a postscript to his translation of that work he endorsed Gourmont's thesis that sex and thinking were two aspects of one process: "The brain itself is, in origin and development, only a sort of great clot of genital fluid . . . . [this] would explain the enormous content of the brain as a maker or presenter of images." [23] This belief, Pound's own version of "Unity of Being," connects the light of enlightenment as well as the "hard light and clear edges" of Imagism with the sexual function—another reason, perhaps, why so many of Pound's poems involve sexual encounters.

The second assumption of this argument is simply the general condition of the first, that "man is—the sensitive physical part of him—a mechanism, for the purpose of our further discussion a mechanism rather like an electric appliance, switches, wires, etc.," or more exactly, like a telegraph, capable of "registering movements in the invisible aether." Refining his senses in a "love-cult" that uses the "charged poles" of opposite sexes, he becomes an instrument of extraordinary sexual registrations; similarly, he can turn himself open to "the vital universe, to the tree and the living rock," for "we have about us the universe of fluid force, and below us the germinal universe of wood alive, of stone alive." This Upwardian conception of a universe full of vital forces enabled Pound to account for the kind of mind that could discern and respond to Luminous Details; the senses in some people can be attuned to these forces and register them. These are the people on whom nothing is lost, as Henry James would say; we might call them human seismographs—the word is used in a related sense in *Mauberley*. They are the artists, people with exteriorized sensibilities, "ever at the interpretation of this vital

---

[22] *Ibid.*, 94. George Dekker, in *Sailing After Knowledge*, 46, uses the passage to make a similar point.

[23] Remy de Gourmont, *The Natural Philosophy of Love*, trans. Ezra Pound (New York, 1922), 206.

universe" by perceiving what is in the air "at greater intensity, and more intimately" than other people.[24]

Pound's whole theory of knowledge presupposes this kind of mind. He talked about "direct knowledge" in a very down-to-earth and de-mystified manner at times, during the Imagist years and later, but always in the background was this residue of mysticism. It colors his idea of myth, and hence his idea of poetry, and hence his idea of "the tradition." The connections among these several topics may be made by citing passages from *Guide to Kulchur*, where Pound was concerned to present his beliefs in their least mystical form. The central link of these connections is in Pound's statement that "the value of Leo Frobenius to civilization" was inherent in the German anthropologist's emphasis on a kind of *real* knowledge preserved in myth, folklore, and oral tradition:

He has in especial seen and marked out a kind of knowing, the difference between knowledge that has to be acquired by particular effort and knowing that is in people, "in the air." He has accented the value of such record. His archaeology is not retrospective, it is immediate.

Example: the peasants opposed a railway cutting. A king had driven into the ground at that place. The engineers dug and unearthed the bronze car of Dis, two thousand years buried.[25]

Earlier in the book Pound for a similar point quoted advice from Fenollosa: we should, like scientists, examine "collections of fact, phenomena, specimens" in order to gather "general equations of real knowledge from them, even though the observed data had no syllogistic connection one with another," and to illustrate this process Pound used his own acquisition of a "form-colour" sense, "a certain real knowledge which wd. enable me to tell a Goya from a Velasquez."

24 *The Spirit of Romance*, 92–94, 87.
25 *Guide to Kulchur*, 57.

Coming even closer to things committed verbally to our memory. There are passages of the poets which approximate the form-colour acquisition.

And herein is clue to Confucius' reiterated commendation of such of his students as studied the Odes.

He demanded or commended a type of perception, a kind of transmission of knowledge obtainable only from such concrete manifestation. Not without reason.[26]

The Confucian attitude toward the *Odes* exemplifies Fenollosa's advice to examine seemingly disparate materials to gather "general equations of real knowledge." In the collection occur layers of such "real knowledge," as in an archaeological site. The *Odes* or any body of true tradition are middens of significant factual details: thus we find Homer's geography and anatomy accurate. For Pound this concept underwrites his own attempt to give the "news that is still news" in the *Cantos,* as well as his belief that the art of poetry is typological, consisting of real historical registrations that form "a living art, an art changing and developing, always the same at root, never the same in appearance for two decades in succession." Hueffer had forced him to admit that the use of tradition must be direct, not derivative: a poet must not record his "emotion at receiving the experience of the emotions of former writers," but must recognize that "Paolo and Francesca loved and suffered precisely as love and suffer the inhabitants of the flat above him." Vital tradition is capable of making the dead live, of making it new (or giving us, in Eliot's phrase, a sense not "of the pastness of the past but of its presence"), because it is made by "donative" authors out of Luminous Details expressing "direct knowledge," particulars presenting universals that cannot be worn away by time.[27]

[26] *Ibid.,* 27–28.

[27] Eliot's phrase is of course from "Tradition and the Individual Talent," which first appeared in the *Egoist* in 1919; see *Selected Essays* (new ed.; New York, 1950), 4. For the Hueffer quotations, see notes 31 and 35 to Chap. One. For Pound's remark, see note 20 to Chap. Three.

Because this idea is so fundamental to Pound, it is necessary to go back to "Psychology and Troubadours" to examine its early manifestations in more detail. The important point to be made is that Pound does not think of mysticism, such as he finds in the Troubadours, as bodiless transmission of vague visions. He wrote of such cultists that for them "ecstasy is not a whirl or a madness of the senses, but a glow arising from the exact nature of the perception." Even of mystic visions Pound predicated exactness, precision, definition as the life-giving component. It was in this essay that Pound proclaimed that "hyper-scientific precision" *alone* gives any matter "immortality," whether it be "of Love appearing in an ash-grey vision, or of the seemingly slight matter of birds and branches." [28] The great example is clearly Dante: "Dante's precision both in the *Vita Nuova* and in the *Commedia* comes from the attempt to reproduce exactly the thing which has been clearly seen. The 'Lord of terrible aspect' is no abstraction, no figure of speech." [29] Pound's comments on the Middle Ages ceaselessly reiterate that they teach a lesson of precision. In *How to Read* and *Guide to Kulchur* he frequently praised medieval "exactness"; he even spoke of their "exact psychology": to Hulme he mentioned "the difference between [Cavalcanti's] precise interpretive metaphor, and the Petrarchan fustian and ornament, pointing out that Guido thought in accurate terms; that the phrases correspond to definite sensations undergone." [30] In "Prolegomena" he suggested that the new mode he was calling for in twentieth-century poetry might well look back to the Middle Ages: "In the art of Daniel and Cavalcanti, I have seen that precision which I miss in the Victorians, that explicit rendering, be it of external nature, or of emotion. Their testimony is of the eyewitness, their symptoms are first

28 *The Spirit of Romance*, 87–88, and 91.
29 *Ibid.*, 126.
30 *Literary Essays*, 21–22, 162; *Guide to Kulchur*, 315.

hand." [31] Very possibly "the glow arising from the exact nature of the perception" was in the back of his mind when he wrote that Imagist "presentation" gives a sense "of sudden liberation . . . from time limits and space limits; that sense of sudden growth, which we experience in the presence of the greatest works of art." This mystic belief in the possibilities of precision in poetry is one of the firmest rooted parts of his poetics.

It is true that for a while Pound tried to compromise the principle of precision by finding a place for the opposed technique of "vague suggestion." This seems to have been the result—natural enough at the time he was entertaining esoteric ideas from people like Mead and Upward—of trying to catch the spirit of "how Yeats did it." As we have seen, Yeats's technique was the type of *symboliste* "atmospheric suggestion" in Pound's mind, specifically contrasted to the "definiteness" of Dante. When he was thinking along mystical lines that Yeats would have approved, he predictably tried to mute the hostility between suggestion and definiteness, as in this passage from an essay of 1911:

When I say that technique is the means of conveying an exact impression of exactly what one means, I do not by any means mean that poetry is to be stripped of any of its powers of vague suggestion. Our life is, in so far as it is worth living, made up in great part of things indefinite, impalpable; and it is precisely because the arts present us these things that we—humanity—cannot get on without the arts. The picture that suggests indefinite poems, the line of verse that means a gallery of paintings . . . it is these things that touch us nearly that "matter." [32]

But Pound could never really acquire a taste for "indefinite poems," and the effort aborted. This mode, as the last sentence shows, implied for him the use of derivative inspirations, and it

[31] *Literary Essays,* 11.
[32] "On Technique," 298.

correlates with a phrase he used to characterize Yeats's poetics: "Works of art beget works of art." But this attitude was exactly what he had to rid himself of in order to acquire a living tradition instead of a derivative, antiquarian one. Hueffer taught him —slowly and painfully—that he could never write great poetry until he captured "living language," and that he could never do this until he abandoned the practice of using "the speech of books and poems that one has read." The effort to swallow "suggestiveness" left some traces, but most faded fairly fast in the wake of Hueffer's insistence on stripping words of all association to get a precise meaning.

Another point to be gleaned from "Psychology and Troubadours" is that Pound was aware of a long occult tradition behind the idea of mind he employed there. This tradition was probably outlined for him by Mead, who was gathering material that was to appear in his *Doctrine of the Subtle Body in Western Tradition*. This work summarizes ancient conceptions of the *sensorium*, a perceptive apparatus not limited to the gross physical body nor severed from it, but extending outward from it into the "vital universe." Mead tries to find a common ground for ancient and modern postulations of an "intimate correspondence between man's psychical and sensible apparatus, or his inner embodiment, and the subtle nature of the universe." [33] Mead's "subtle" universe is similar to Upward's universe of "fluid force"; it implies many existences not immaterial but of an order of corporeality too fine for the gross senses to perceive. This conception stuck in Pound's mind: in *Guide to Kulchur* he spoke of "God and soul, not immaterial '*noos*' (mind) but more subtle corporeal substances." [34] (For the explication of the "blood rite" in Canto I it should be noted that Mead reports a

[33] G. R. S. Mead, *The Doctrine of the Subtle Body in Western Tradition* (London, 1919), 12.
[34] *Guide to Kulchur*, 123.

theory that blood is the "vehicle" for the operations of the *sensorium.*) In alchemical times the "subtle" body was supposed to be mostly air, as the physical body was supposed to be mostly earth, and it was thought to live on after the dissolution of the physical: "After death it was known as the image *(eidōlon, image, simulacrum)* or shade *(skia, umbra)*." [35] Yeats's use of the word "image" in "Byzantium" evidently reflects his own study of this tradition.

There is an obvious link between Pound's speculation that the Troubadours achieved an " 'exteriorization of sensibility,' and interpretation of the cosmos by feeling," and Mead's conclusion that "the physical body of man is as it were the exteriorization of an invisible subtle embodiment of the life of the mind." [36] More specifically, Pound outlined in his "Medievalism" essay on Cavalcanti a view of an aesthetic sensorium that seems to draw on Mead's work:

The Tuscan demands harmony in something more than the plastic. He declines to limit his aesthetic to the impact of light on the eye . . . . This really complicates the aesthetic. You deal with an interactive force: the *virtu* in short.
And dealing with it is not anti-life. It is not maiming, it is not curtailment. The senses at first seem to project for a few yards beyond the body. Effect of a decent climate where a man leaves his nerve-set open, or allows it to tune in to its ambience . . . . The conception of the body as perfect instrument of the increasing intelligence pervades.[37]

Pound remarked that we may, if we wish, describe such exteriorized or projected perception in a graceless terminology as "aesthetic or interactive vasomotor magnetism in relation to the

---

[35] *Doctrine of the Subtle Body,* 49.
[36] *Ibid.,* 1.
[37] "Medievalism," first published in the *Dial* (1928) and then in Pound's edition of Cavalcanti (1932) and in *Make it New* (1934); see *Literary Essays,* 151–55.

consciousness"; but really the idea is alien to our times, for there
has been a great falling off, a loss of faith in our bodies that is
reflected in the art of Raphael and Rubens: "The metamorphosis
into carnal tissue becomes frequent and general somewhere
about 1527. The people are corpus, corpuscular, but not in the
strict sense 'animate,' it is no longer the body of air clothed in
the body of fire; it no longer radiates, light no longer moves
from the eye, there is a great deal of meat . . . . The dinner scene
is more frequently introduced." Since this fall we have become
excessively flesh-centered, or in blind reaction we make the opposite mistake of asceticism; in either case we no longer culti-
vate our *sensoria* or exteriorize our sensibilities. Hence we find
it hard even to imagine what was clearly evident to Cavalcanti:

> We appear to have lost the radiant world where one thought
> cuts through another with clean edge, a world of moving ener-
> gies *"mezzo oscuro rade," "risplende in sè perpetuale effecto,"*
> magnetisms that take form, that are seen, or that border the
> visible, the matter of Dante's *paradiso,* the glass under water, the
> form that seems a form seen in a mirror, these realities percep-
> tible to the sense, interacting . . . . this "harmony in the sentience"
> or harmony *of* the sentient, where the thought has its demarca-
> tion, the substance its *virtu,* where stupid men have not reduced
> all "energy" to unbounded undistinguished abstraction.

Among other things this passage is an ingenious assertion that
visionary activity leads to greater precision, not less, in perception and presentation. It is followed by a denunciation of modern thought for tolerating imprecise and formless concepts of
energy: for us energy "has no borders, it is a shapeless 'mass' of
force," whereas "the medieval philosopher would probably have
been unable to think the electric world, and *not* think of it as a
world of forms." The inseparability of force and form is a cardi-
nal principle for Pound, and the basis of Vorticist theory, which
will be discussed later. Altogether Pound's obsession with "exact

definition" pervades this essay, providing further elucidation of the concern in his poetry for "shapes" of experience, and all their concomitants: sharp outlines, "hard-edgedness," precise terminology, and scorn of blurry effects. A morphology of experience requires clear distinctions and separations—fittingly Pound finds his model in the Middle Ages. He did not object to what later ages scorned as pedantic fussiness about terms, or rigidities of hierarchical thinking, in medieval writers: to his mind these were all to the good, since they preserved demarcations, gradations, and values with exactness.

At about the time he was putting his ideas into "Psychology and Troubadours," Pound was also writing a poem called "The Flame," which somewhat overexplicitly records the same belief in the mystical possibilities of sex. " 'Tis not a game that plays at mates and mating,/ Provence knew," it begins.

> We who are wise beyond your dream of wisdom,
> Drink our immortal moments: we "pass through."
> We have gone forth beyond your bonds and borders,
> Provence knew;
> And all the tales of Oisin say but this:
> That man doth pass the net of days and hours.
>
> .   .   .   .   .   .
>
> There *is* the subtler music, the clear light
> Where time burns back about th' eternal embers.
> We are not shut from all the thousand heavens:
> Lo, there are many gods whom we have seen.

And so on. It is not a very good poem, being tinged with pre-Imagist faults, but it is a very important one. It points forward in its last lines to the final section of *Near Perigord:*

> Search not my lips, O Love, let go my hands,
> This thing that moves as man is no more mortal.

If thou hast seen my shade sans character,
If thou hast seen that mirror of all moments,
That glass to all things that o'ershadow it,
Call not that mirror me, for I have slipped
Your grasp, I have eluded.

The image of Maent as "a shifting change,/ A broken bundle of mirrors" in the later poem is drawn from similar speculations about the mystery of personality and self-transcendence. Some persons can, as it were, "pass through" and beyond the bounds of their limited selves—as did the Troubadours, through their mystic discipline. The mystery of personality is another of the obsessive topics of Pound's poetry, like the forces of sex: the most obvious example is "On His Own Face in a Glass," which also uses the mirror image. In other poems, like "The Tomb at Akr Çaar," Pound muses on self and soul in a way that reminds us that Mead, Upward, and Pound's mystical speculations were part of a Yeatsian ambience. (Let us not forget the appearance of Oisin in "The Flame.") In fact, all of Pound's poems are in a way concerned with this problem:

In the "search for oneself," in the search for "sincere self-expression," one gropes, one finds some seeming verity. One says "I am" this, that, or the other, and with the words scarcely uttered one ceases to be that thing.
     I began this search for the real in a book called *Personae*, casting off, as it were, complete masks of the self in each poem. I continued in long series of translations, which were but more elaborate masks.[38]

Further implications of this statement will appear later; here the point is simply that Pound's own trying-out of identities conditioned the problem of personality in a general sense as it occurs in the poems. It helps to understand that the passage above is not

[38] *Gaudier-Brzeska*, 85. (From the 1914 "Vorticism" essay.)

a confession of the usual adolescent identity crisis, but reflects as does "The Flame" the projection of awareness and transcendence of the limited self or "personality": if we believe that our senses can project out from the body into a "subtle" or "vital" universe, we will hardly be satisfied with everyday ideas of our own identity. We may well try to "be"other people; did not Keats insist that the poet takes on the character of his subject?

There is a clear continuity between the ideas of "Psychology and Troubadours" and Pound's beliefs about myth. One line in "The Flame" suggests the link: "Lo, there are many gods whom we have seen." If a mind is open to the vital universe, its apprehensions may take the form of visions of gods. Asked for his religious affiliation in a hospital, Pound called himself an acceptor of "Greek deities," and elsewhere began a *credo:* "I assert that the Gods exist. . . . I assert that a great treasure of verity exists for mankind in Ovid and in the subject matter of Ovid's long poem, and that only in this form could it be registered." [39] This was not a bit of hoopla to enliven the *Guide to Kulchur,* for he had put it just as emphatically to Harriet Monroe many years before: "Say that I consider the Writings of Confucius, and Ovid's *Metamorphoses* the only safe guides in religion . . . . that I refuse to accept ANY monotheistic taboos whatsoever. That I consider the *Metamorphoses* a sacred book." [40] I doubt if we have the right to assume that Pound was not utterly serious here, for his belief is a natural consequence of all his thinking about religion. A passage from "Psychology and Troubadours" shows it forming:

I believe in a sort of permanent basis in humanity, that is to say, I believe that Greek myth arose when someone having passed through delightful psychic experience tried to communicate it to others and found it necessary to screen himself from persecu-

[39] *Guide to Kulchur,* 301, 299.
[40] *Letters,* 183.

tion. Speaking aesthetically, the myths are explications of mood: you may stop there, or you may probe deeper. Certain it is that these myths are only intelligible in a vivid and glittering sense to those people to whom they occur. I know, I mean, one man who understands Persephone and Demeter, and one who understands the Laurel, and another who has, I should say, met Artemis. These things are for them *real*.[41]

The last sentence is of course the essential one. It is consistent with his warning prefaced to the statement that Dante's "Lord of terrible aspect" was "no abstraction, no figure of speech": "Anyone who has in any degree the faculty of vision will know that the so-called personifications are real and not artificial. . . . There are some who can not or will not understand these things." [42] By "faculty of vision" Pound seems to have meant something more than two eyes in working order.

In "Psychology and Troubadours" Pound credits myth to a kind of mind even more sensitive to the "vital universe" than that of the Troubadours.

The consciousness of some [Troubadour poets] seems to rest, or have its center more properly, in what the Greek psychologists called the *phantastikon*. Their minds are, that is, circumvolved about them like soap-bubbles reflecting sundry patches of the macrocosmos. And with certain others their consciousness is "germinal." Their thoughts are in them as the thought of the tree is in the seed, or in the grass, or the grain, or the blossom. And these minds are the more poetic, and they affect mind about them, and transmute it as the seed the earth. And this latter sort of mind is close on the vital universe; and the strength of the Greek beauty rests in this, that it is ever at the interpretation of this vital universe, by its signs of gods and godly attendants and oreads.[43]

Pound had probably not at this time read Fenollosa's essay, yet

[41] *The Spirit of Romance*, 92.
[42] *Ibid.*, 126.
[43] *Ibid.*, 92–93.

his very phrases seem to recall the progression of Fenollosa's argument from his thesis about "relations" to his view of the nature of myth: "Relations are more real and more important than the things which they relate. The forces which produce the branch-angles of an oak lay potent in the acorn. . . . Metaphor, the revealer of nature, is the very substance of poetry. The known interprets the obscure, the universe is alive with myth." Myth for Fenollosa was the most concentrated development of metaphor, "the use of material images to suggest immaterial relations." A universe in which immaterial relations are the most real and important things is very like a vital or subtle "universe of fluid force"; Fenollosa said nothing about a *sensorium* or *phantastikon*, but ascribed interpretative and preservative functions to language itself:

Metaphor, its [poetry's] chief device, is at once the substance of nature and of language. Poetry only does consciously what the primitive races did unconsciously. The chief work of literary men in dealing with language, and of poets especially, lies in feeling back along the ancient lines of advance. . . . poetry was the earliest of the world arts; poetry, language and the care of myth grew up together. . . . Our ancestors built the accumulations of metaphor into structures of language and into systems of thought.[44]

To this particular argument for the importance of myth and poetic tradition Pound subscribed a footnote: "I would submit in all humility that this applies in the rendering of ancient texts. The poet in dealing with his own time, must also see to it that language does not petrify on his hands. He must prepare for new advances along the lines of true metaphor that is interpretative metaphor, or image, as diametrically opposed to untrue, or ornamental metaphor." This is a useful note on Pound's translation habits and on the differentiation of image from explanatory

[44] See note 48 to Chap. Two.

metaphor, but its relevance here is in Pound's easy acceptance of Fenollosa's view of myth. Obviously the kind of underpinning that Fenollosa gave to Pound's "tradition" was different from that given by Mead and Upward, yet the two sources converge in an overview of a body of "interpretation of the vital universe" preserved in the ancient texts. "Interpretative" (sometimes "interpretive") was Pound's name for the function that "is the highest honor of the arts." [45] This function is the criterion not only for "the tradition" but also for modern poetry: in his own work as well as in translation the poet must use true "interpretative metaphor" that feels along the lines of the vital forces or, in Fenollosa's words, "objective lines of relations" in the universe—the "language of exploration." Only by using this kind of more-than-metaphor can the poet achieve "hyperscientific precision"; the two are interdependent, and together form the substance of a "poetry of reality" best represented in myth.

It may be inferred from such passages as the above that Pound believed modern poets capable of creating myth in their own right. But he identified himself more often with the Troubadours or Tuscans than with the Greeks, operating not at such creative voltage as to produce myth but getting a similar "interpretative" effect by the use of the *phantastikon*. One stanza of "The Condolence," part of the "Contemporania" series, addresses the poems themselves:

> O my fellow sufferers, we went out under the trees,
> We were in especial bored with male stupidity,
> We went forth gathering delicate thoughts,
> Our "*fantastikon*" delighted to serve us.

---

[45] *The Spirit of Romance*, 87. Pound's use of the word perhaps derives from early reading of Matthew Arnold; cf. Arnold's essay on Maurice de Guérin: "The grand power of poetry is its interpretative power . . ." etc.

We were not exasperated with women,
for the female is ductile.

Perhaps Pound practiced a mild form of the "love-cult," seeking registrations of those immaterial forces. Unlike his friends Hulme and Wyndham Lewis, Pound never expressed the sweeping contempt for women that, as Charles Norman says, "always accompanies authoritarian reveries."[46] In fact Pound's sexual imagery sets him off from his contemporaries in several ways: Eliot, more hurt by the world, dwells on rape, desecration, sordid consenting, or on highly oblique fertility images (water, "a slotted window bellied like the fig's fruit," and "brown hair over the mouth blown"); these, even in their promise of renewal, are cruel betrayals into painful life (April strips us of "forgetful snow," "depraved May" brings "flowering judas"). Yeats manages to combine, often enough, a sense of violation, bestiality, and triumph. But Pound's sexual imagery is more straightforward, more cavalier, and honors fertility without compromise. He would seem to have seen greater potentialities in "love-cults." The differentiation extends to the use of mythological material: Tiresias typifies Eliot, Leda represents Yeats, but Pound is concerned with Aphrodite.

Pound's cultivation of the *phantastikon* did not imply that he thought myth banished from our world, however. In an essay on the musician Arnold Dolmetsch (which begins "I have seen the God Pan"), Pound defined myth in terms that suggest that we can recover what only seems lost by eschewing certain reductive habits:

The undeniable tradition of metamorphoses teaches us that things do not remain always the same. They become other things by swift and unanalysable process. It was only when men began to mistrust the myths and to tell nasty lies about the Gods

[46] Norman, *Ezra Pound*, 175.

for a moral purpose that these matters became hopelessly confused. Then some unpleasing Semite or Parsee or Syrian began to use myths for social propaganda, when the myth was degraded into an allegory or a fable, and that was the beginning of the end. And the Gods no longer walked in men's gardens. The first myths arose when a man walked sheer into "nonsense," that is to say, when some very vivid and undeniable adventure befell him, and he told someone else who called him a liar. Thereupon, after bitter experience, perceiving that no one could understand what he meant when he said that he "turned into a tree" he made a myth—a work of art that is—an impersonal or objective story woven out of his own emotion, as the nearest equation that he was capable of putting into words. That story, perhaps, then gave rise to a weaker copy of his emotion in others, until there arose a cult, a company of people who could understand each other's nonsense about the gods.[47]

It is no longer possible to have myth created in just that way, of course; any "cult" today would have to be too self-conscious. What then does Pound think we can have?

Many literary comparisons have been proposed for the *Cantos:* Homer and Dante obviously, lately and suggestively *Piers Plowman,* and perhaps we should add Blake's Prophetic Books. But the best analogy of all is surely Ovid's *Metamorphoses,* a work that Pound seems unable to praise too much. Ovid, however, was not "writing" mythology, but rather constructing a living compendium of myth, gathering together metamorphic interpretations of realities. So also with Pound, who retells certain vital segments of myth, flashes of man's intercourse with the "vital universe," rendering them in his own "interpretative metaphors." Like Fenollosa he believes in language carrying alluvial deposits of these meanings, hence his interest in the layers of language, e.g., in various translations of Homer. Those layers preserve live speech, on the importance of which Hueffer, Fenollosa, and Frobenius agree. Its importance is not diminished by

[47] "Arnold Dolmetsch," *New Age,* XVI (1915), 246; reprinted in *Pavannes and Divisions* (1918); see *Literary Essays,* 431.

literacy or the advance of culture: "The spoken idiom is not only a prime factor, but certainly one of the most potent, progressively so as any modality of civilization ages." [48] In the later Cantos Pound makes use of the term "Sagetrieb, or the oral tradition," and plainly means it to apply to his poem: "There is no mystery about the Cantos, they are the tale of the tribe—give Rudyard credit for his use of the phrase." [49] Trying to convince prospective readers that the poem was not a *tour de force* of polyglot scholia, he stated: "There *is* at start, descent to the shades, metamorphoses, parallel (Vidal-Actaeon). All of which is mere matter for little . . . . rs and Harvud instructors *unless* I pull it off as reading matter, singing matter, shouting matter, the tale of the tribe." [50] Though he did not care for Mallarmé, he has plainly attempted to give a more pure sense to the words of the tribe, filing with his Imagist precision the tropes and images that serve as his Luminous Details, but always remembering the oral source.

With his "Sagetrieb" Pound was trying to overcome a serious handicap in the way of modern understanding of mythology; this is the ingrained assumption that creation must be "original" and "individual," that the author cannot make use of his material in its primitive form but must make it conform to his personal pattern. But a "cult of personality" violates the whole spirit of mythology, which is communal or cultic rather than individual. The high-water mark of the age of myth, in Pound's eyes, was the institution of the Eleusinian mysteries, which provided integration into a community (although it did not, like less moderate mysticisms, allow the individual to sink into an "unconditioned ground of being"). For Pound "our time has overshadowed the mysteries by an overemphasis on the individual. . . . Eleusis did

---

[48] "Date Line," first printed in *Make it New* (1934); see *Literary Essays*, 77.
[49] Canto LXXXIX; *Guide to Kulchur*, 194.
[50] *Letters*, 294.

not distort truth by exaggerating the individual, neither could
it have violated the individual spirit." [51] The extension of the
view of myth as communal is that "literature rises in racial process" and should express what Frobenius called *Kulturmorpho-
logie* rather than individual "creativity." So Pound in aiming at
the "tale of the tribe" was bound to leave himself open to the
suspicion that he lacked originality; it was a risk he was prepared
to run in order to get the "spoken tradition" onto paper.

Pound believed that his poem was being written at that point
in history when it was possible to extricate myth from the
pigeonhole of "fable and allegory" at last, thanks to the insights
of men like Frobenius who saw in it a "reality" beyond the usual
definitions of that term. In one of the passages in *Guide to Kulchur* asserting that "the gods exist," he remarks that "it has taken
two thousand years to get round again to meditating on mythology." [52] Yet the implication is present in Pound's arguments
that the knowledge has been in the air all along, borne on the
stream of tradition. Gemisthus Plethon and John Heydon,
among others, knew what we know. Fortunately for Pound's
purpose, the Christian Neo-Platonics were in the habit of taking
pagan myth seriously, as one more set of hieroglyphics by which
God revealed truth to the world. [53] So he found many precedents
for such statements as "I assert that a great treasure of verity
exists for mankind in Ovid."

Ovid's great work provides yet another major analogue to the
art of the *Cantos* in its organization. Pound never assumed that
unity was Ovid's aim, but rather took the *Metamorphoses* to be

---

[51] *Guide to Kulchur*, 299. A true work of communal myth is of course
"poetry of reality"; cf. Canto XCIX: "This is not a work of fiction/nor
yet of one man." Also note his remark in "Prolegomena": "It is tremen-
dously important that great poetry be written, it makes no jot of difference who writes it" (*Literary Essays*, p. 10).
[52] *Guide to Kulchur*, 125.
[53] Gombrich, "*Icones Symbolicae*," 169.

a compendium of its varied sources and insights, multi-layered and multi-faceted. Pound was alert to the signs of various strata preserved in the great traditional works; in the *Odyssey* he saw the journey to Hades as the primal layer: "The Nekuia shouts aloud that it is *older* than the rest, all that island, Cretan, etc., hinter-time." [54] Following this line of thought he concluded that the whole idea of unity had been distorted: "I suspect neither Homer nor Dante *had* the kind of boring 'unity' of surface that we take to be characteristic of Pope, Racine, Corneille." [55] He even began to suspect that Homer's apparent unity might be the result of tampering by editors, and reinforced his suspicion by musing on works of tradition whose permanence is certainly not due to any " 'unity' of surface":

Pisistratus found the Homeric texts in disorder, we don't quite know what he did about it. The Bible is a compendium, people trimmed it to make it solid. It has gone on for ages, because it wasn't allowed to overrun all the available parchment . . . . Ovid's Metamorphoses are a compendium, not an epic like Homer's; Chaucer's Canterbury Tales are a compendium of all the good yarns Chaucer knew. The Tales have lasted through centuries while the long-winded medieval narratives went into museums.[56]

It should be pointed out that these remarks are the substance of the page of the *ABC of Reading* devoted to the "DICHTEN= CONDENSARE" principle. Pound apparently believes that if a poet really concentrates his work, the logical result is a compendium; a long unified tale can be produced only by spreading the effort. He assumes that the immortality of his illustrative works is due to such concentration. The list of examples might be extended, with the Confucian Odes for instance; the applicability to the *Cantos* is obvious.

[54] *Letters*, 274.
[55] *Ibid.*
[56] *ABC of Reading*, 92.

If a poet proposes to himself to write not a "myth for our time" but a huge process-epic carrying the burden of a "tradition" embodied in various layers of language and racial consciousness, how could his work be anything other than a compendium? Various phrases are now coming into use to suggest the new conventions that Pound and other modernists have utilized: composition by field, diffusion as organization, and others. But for Pound's work the root of the matter is that real concentration boils a work down to separate "gists and piths," which must seem at first fragmentary and disunified. He has never desired a unity of surface or style, nor made a secret of the "binding matter" in the *Cantos* which, while holding the poem together, has made it seem even more heterogeneous. This matter includes, for instance, annotations: "Part of the job is *finally* to get all the necessary notes into the text itself. Not only are the LI Cantos a part of the poem, but by labeling most of 'em draft, I retain right to include *necessary* explanations in LI-C or in revision." He added in explanation of this procedure that "Binyon has shown that Dante needs *fewer* notes than are usually given the student," the implication being that Dante too worked his notes into the text.[57] Insofar as Pound really hoped to write "the tale of the tribe" his work must be endless, episodic, and conglomerate, justifying itself only in the sharp etching of those bits of fact that "govern knowledge as the switchboard governs an electric circuit." The very precision demanded in the etching of those details prevents them from being subordinated to any unifying principle; tonal or thematic unity imposed by a single mind, no matter how creative, tends to diminish the sense of jagged clarity. If the texture is made smooth, the details cannot stand out sharply. As we have seen, Pound suspects that there has been some homogenizing of Homer's surface, so that only now are we beginning to notice just how clearly and ac-

[57] *Letters,* 293.

curately his details preserve the knowledge of his time. The ancient Greeks must have seen more than "a good story" in Homer, to make him the basis of their educational system.

Thus, though the *Cantos* have plenty of "themes" and "links," everything is not subordinated to them, and Pound never seeks the kind of imposed external form that would make his work seem more readily graspable. A clear idea of his values and predilections in this area can be found in his defense of the work of William Carlos Williams, another believer in living language:

> Very well, he does not "conclude"; his work has been "often formless," "incoherent," opaque, obscure, obfuscated, confused, truncated, etc. . . . But it can do us no harm to stop an hour or so and consider the number of very important chunks of world-literature in which form, major form, is remarkable mainly for absence [such as the *Iliad*, Aeschylus' *Prometheus*, Montaigne, Rabelais, *Bouvard and Pécuchet*].
>
> The component of these great works and *the* indispensable component is texture; which Dr. Williams indubitably has in the best, and in increasingly frequent, passages of his writing.[58]

The *Cantos* too seek texture rather than major form. In this case Pound was arguing not merely from a technical point of view, but from a religious or metaphysical one, from a belief that the polytheistic, metamorphic character of oral and epic tradition necessitates "formlessness." He remarks in paragraphs that immediately precede the defense of Williams' work:

[58] "Dr. Williams' Position" (see note 65 to Chap. One); *Literary Essays*, 394–95. The "structural study" of myth now being proposed by Lévi-Strauss and other anthropologists concentrates on "vertical" and repetitive aspects, obviating ideas of "form" based on "horizontal" linear progressions such as plot, character development, and the like. Thus we are now doubly able to see myth as a source for the "spatial form" that inheres in the *Cantos*. See Claude Lévi-Strauss, "The Structural Study of Myth," in *Myth: A Symposium*, ed. Thomas A. Sebeok, Midland ed. (Bloomington and London, 1965), 81–106. Lévi-Strauss also remarks, in *The Savage Mind* (Chicago, 1966), 18, that "the elements of mythical thought similarly lie half-way between percepts and concepts." As I have pointed out, this is a characteristic of Pound's "Image" also.

We are still so generally obsessed by monism and monotheistical backwash, and ideas of orthodoxy that we (and the benighted Britons) can hardly observe a dissociation of ideas without thinking a censure is somehow therein implied . . . . as if monism or monotheism were anything more than a hypothesis agreeable to certain types of very lazy minds too weak to bear an uncertainty or to remain in "uncertainty."

The use of Keats's "negative capability" principle can only have been meant to imply that the same weakness that chooses monotheism to assuage its uncertainties is also responsible for the over-emphasis on tidy and symmetrical forms. Williams, for Pound a salient example of "racial process" in literature, is credited with "Mediterranean equipment," which puts him in the line with the other great "Mediterranean" artists, from Homer to Flaubert, who have created "formless" works; Pound clearly believes that the natural polytheism of Mediterranean myth is racially ingrained in these artists, and that it accounts for their heterogeneity. In Pound's thinking on myth the stress is always on "many gods," diversities of insight, and varieties of presentation. Very possibly his adverse reaction to Milton's imposition of Latinate form on his material was part of a deeper reaction against what he would feel to be a restricted religious insight.

When asked anxious questions about the form of the *Cantos*, Pound's replies usually tried to indicate that the poem was not schematic, but organic in the most literal sense—growing: "As to the *form* of *The Cantos:* All I can say or pray is: *wait* till it's there. I mean wait till I get 'em written and then if it don't show, I will start exegesis. I haven't an Aquinas-map; Aquinas *not* valid now." [59] Some critics have read this to mean that somehow, at the end, out of a hat, Pound was going to try to come up with a principle that would run backwards and make order where there was only chaos before. Such critics tend to sit back with an air

[59] *Letters*, 323.

of triumph as the poem grows. But since the whole idea of imposed form goes against everything Pound has stood for, I suggest we take literally his advice not to look for the hidden Aquinas-map. What he did expect, probably, was that the *Sagetrieb* would show more clearly at the end. This is not to say that the *Cantos* are an aleatoric "action painting," of course. Pound has never been willing to discard the values of intelligence and consciousness: he likened creative effort without intellectual control to a railway engine without tracks.[60] It is not likely that his habits of composition were so literally scatterbrained as the "action painting" analogy implies; and in his Vorticist writings he derided "automatism."

Study of Pound's writings has convinced me that even by the most hostile evaluation his mind was never so disorganized as to prevent him from imposing "form" on the *Cantos* if he had wanted to. It rather seems that his principles of composition were governed by two great values he derived from "the tradition"— medieval exact distinctions and Ovidian multiplicity. It can even be demonstrated that these two poles of his tradition had for him a connection:

I cannot repeat too often that there was a profound psychological knowledge in medieval Provence, however Gothic its expression; that men, concentrated on certain validities, attaining an exact and diversified terminology, have there displayed considerable penetration; that this was carried into early Italian poetry; and faded from it when metaphors became decorative instead of interpretative; and that the age of Aquinas would not have tolerated sloppy expression of psychology concurrent with the exact expression of "mysticism." There is also great wisdom in Ovid.[61]

The connection of course is in the belief that precise and vital

[60] *Literary Essays,* 71.
[61] *Ibid.,* 344. (From the essay on Remy de Gourmont of 1920.)

language and detail, as in Cavalcanti, Ovid, or the "spoken tradition" generally, can preserve knowledge even of a highly esoteric order.

That tradition-derived values such as precision, "Luminous Detail," and the like accord with Imagist principles will, I hope, readily be granted. But there is an even deeper relationship between Imagist ideas and those which find their first articulation in "Psychology and Troubadours," having to do with the use of visions. We are now coming to recognize that large parts of the *Cantos* are records of visionary activity. Robert Fitzgerald recorded on a visit to Rapallo that Pound dropped the remark " 'I live in music for days at a time.' He did not mean the wordless music of the composers—Vivaldi, Antheil—who then interested him, but the music within himself, a visionary music requiring words. I knew that this applied to the Cantos." [62] I believe that Fitzgerald was right to interpret "music" in this way. This might explain a remark Pound made to Margaret Anderson in 1918: "Chère amie, I am, for the time being, bored to death with being any kind of an editor. I desire to go on with my long poem; and like the Duke of Chang, I desire to hear the music of a lost dynasty. (Have managed to hear it, in fact.)" [63] On the referential level, "music" here might refer to the Provençal sound-values which he was trying to resurrect, but since he always connected that aspect of Troubadour poetry with their penetration of certain secrets of the universe, I am satisfied that the term has a larger sense here, and that the "music" of the *Cantos* has a mystical substratum. Any "visions" Pound may have cultivated would have had words and music as well as

[62] Quoted by Norman, *Ezra Pound*, 310.

[63] *Letters*, 128. At least one of Pound's statements implies that he had been experiencing visions since 1910 or earlier: "No man who has not passed through, or nearly approached that spiritual experience known as illumination—I use the word in a technical sense—can appreciate the *Paradiso* to the full" (*The Spirit of Romance*, 144).

visual registration. The connection with Imagism comes in the fact that at least once Pound defined Imagism so as to lay a heavy emphasis on its visionary potential: he called it "poetry wherein the feelings of painting and sculpture are predominant (certain men move in phantasmagoria; the images of their gods, whole countrysides, stretches of hill and forest, travel with them)." [64] "Phantasmagoria" is presumably that which is produced by the activity of the *phantastikon*, which Pound had been cultivating since 1912.

Pound made the above definition in 1920, very likely as a result of pondering how his Imagist purposes fitted the program for his long poem. But it suggests a perspective for looking back at all Pound's work since 1912, the year that produced both Imagism and "Psychology and Troubadours." This perspective is useful in spite of the fact that Pound did undergo a reaction against the "mushiness" of some mystical thought. I have described elsewhere in some detail the growth of Pound's boredom with Yeats's "psychical research" and his loss of patience with some muzzy forms of Orientalism; but I would add to that account a note that the same letter that makes a derogatory remark about Yeats's spiritualism also contains a recommendation of Upward's *Divine Mystery* and *New Word*.[65] Rejecting the looser mysticism, he cleaved to more "exact" kinds. And there is one final detail that helps reconcile any seeming disparities in his

---

[64] *Instigations of Ezra Pound*, 234. Cf. the remark quoted in the preceding note about illumination and the *Paradiso* with the later statement: "Dante's 'Paradiso' is the most wonderful *image*" (*Gaudier-Brzeska*, 86: from the 1914 "Vorticism" essay). In a letter to Joyce of March 17, 1917 Pound indicated that he thought of the *Cantos* as originally Imagistic or phanopoeic: "I have begun an endless poem, of no known category. Phanopoeia or something or other, all about everything. 'Poetry' may print the first three cantos this spring." See *Pound/Joyce: The Letters of Ezra Pound to James Joyce, with Pound's Essays on Joyce*, ed. Forrest Read (New York, 1967), 102. Read concludes from this statement that "Phanopoeia" was Pound's original provisional title for the *Cantos*.

[65] In "Pound and Yeats: The Question of Symbolism"; cf. *Letters*, 25.

thought on these subjects. In his obituary article on Hueffer,
Pound made a striking revelation: "That Ford was almost an
halluciné few of his intimates can doubt. He felt until it para-
lysed his efficient action, he saw quite distinctly the Venus immortal crossing the tram tracks." [66] If Hueffer, with all his insistence on precise and veridical rendering of realities, could
himself have been given to visionary experience, surely Pound
cannot have felt any conflict between phantasmagoric activities
and his "poetry of reality." He must on the contrary have felt
the profundity of his observation about modern men who have
had visions of gods: "These things are for them *real*."

---

[66] See note 33 to Chap. One.

FIVE

TRADITION AND
TWO INDIVIDUAL TALENTS

Pound and Eliot

FORCE AND FORM

I AM PREPARED to admit that my treatment of "the tradition" assumes deeper affinities between the minds of Pound and Eliot than either would have acknowledged. While the two are generally linked together as founders of modernism, it is easy to show vast divergences in their purposes. But their early alliance was not a matter of chance: there is a clear enough rationale. The most concrete evidence is the record of Pound's shaping spirit on the manuscript of *The Waste Land*. We also have the fact that the two "at a particular date in a particular room . . . decided that the dilutation of *vers libre*, Amygism, Lee Masterism, general floppiness had gone too far, and that some counter-current must be set going": the "remedy" they decided on was "rhyme and regular strophes." [1] Acting more or less in concert they championed Remy de Gourmont, explained Henry James (each contributing to the other's James symposium), and performed other mutual services. Eliot took up many of Pound's

[1] Pound, *Polite Essays*, 14. We do not have *The Waste Land* manuscript in full yet, but see *Letters*, 169–72.

quarrels: into his reviews for the *Egoist* he dropped biting comments on Amygists, Georgians, and other writers Pound scorned as "degrading the values." When Pound in a cold fury printed in his "corner" of the *Little Review* Section 211 of the U.S. Penal Code, prohibiting importation of obscene books, Eliot took it up concurrently in the *Egoist*.[2] This points to more than friendly cooperation, and suggests that their activity was a campaign with agreed-upon objectives.

The most important attack mounted by Eliot in his tenure as assistant editor of the *Egoist* was manifested in the recurrent theme of his series of "Reflections on Contemporary Poetry"— that it was "deficient in tradition." In 1919, just as the *Egoist* expired, he brought out the now-famous "Tradition and the Individual Talent." The records suggest that the essay was meant to strike another blow at the degenerate state of culture and at poetry in England and America, a blow at provincial narrowness and insular complacency. It coincides with Pound's fulminations against the thinness of American intellect, and the smug "petrifaction of mind" in England, both of which resisted his demand for a truly cosmopolitan "tradition." That Pound had as much responsibility for the final shape of the essay as he did for that of *The Waste Land* is impossible, yet the essay's arguments are a subtle and compelling statement of ideas that had already occupied him for a long time. Eliot's originality is not in question, and no doubt his superior philosophical training enabled him to couch the ideas in sounder terms than Pound ever found. But the essay was part of a war that was as much Pound's as Eliot's.

Pound had made "tradition" an open campaign by helping to found the Vorticist movement. The name "Vorticism" itself

---

[2] A month-by-month comparison of the files of the *Egoist* and *Little Review*, 1917–19, can be very enlightening. It rules out the possibility of coincidence.

represented the fruit of his effort to conceptualize a dynamic tradition: it is an emblem of pure form created and maintained by powerful force, and the force that Pound had most in mind was one of "racial process," or culture and tradition. In an article on "Technique" in 1912 he used an involved metaphor of words as electric poles or cones, radiating magnetic lines of force in the same way as do the "poles" of human sexuality in "Psychology and Troubadours." "This peculiar energy which fills the cones is the power of tradition, of centuries of race consciousness, of agreement, of association . . . . three or four words in exact juxtaposition are capable of radiating this energy at a very high potentiality." [3] Such metaphors eventually yielded to the more useful figure of the vortex, which he adopted for the first time in 1913 to designate cities as focusing points for the "peculiar energy" of culture and tradition: London, he wrote, like Rome "is a main and a vortex, drawing strength from the peripheries"; later that year he called London "The Vortex" in a letter to William Carlos Williams.[4] In 1914, searching for a name for the new movement, he realized that "The Vortex" could also stand for a mobile concentration of forces that an artist could bring to bear in his work. In Pound's "vortex" one force predominates: "All experience rushes into this vortex. All the energized past, all the past that is living and worthy to live. ALL MOMENTUM, which is the past bearing upon us, RACE, RACE-MEMORY, instinct charging the PLACID, NON-ENERGIZED FUTURE." [5] The "Great English Vortex" of 1914 was to be a maelstrom of energy held in place and focused by the power of tradition.

That Vorticism was actually a conservative and not a revo-

---

[3] "On Technique," 298. Such metaphors for tradition as the "river" (see note 17 to Chap. Four) also depend on the idea of form maintained by force.

[4] "Through Alien Eyes," *New Age*, XII (1913), 300; *Letters*, 28.

[5] "Vortex. Pound," *Blast* No. 1 (June 20, 1914), 153.

lutionary movement should not be a surprising discovery, given the character of Pound's and Wyndham Lewis' thought. Its manic hostilities obscured this conservatism somewhat, but these befit a movement founded in 1914. The most violent denunciations were directed against "the man in the street," the vulgar mob, *homo canis* as Pound called him; and the Vorticists particularly hated his narrow, negativistic idea of "tradition." Pound differentiated the new movement from those like Futurism that wanted simply to obliterate the past: "The vorticist has not this curious tic for destroying past glories. . . . We do not desire to evade comparison with the past. We prefer that the comparison be made by some intelligent person whose idea of 'the tradition' is not limited by the conventional taste of four or five centuries and one continent." [6]

The Vorticist conception of the ideal artist envisioned him as purged of all desire to please the public, working only to project the force of his "will and consciousness" into his material in such a way as to induce form latent in that material. Pound had a favorite analogy for this process:

An organisation of forms expresses a confluence of forces. These forces may be the "love of God," the "life-force," emotions, passions, what you will. For example: if you clap a strong magnet beneath a plateful of iron filings, the energies of the magnet will proceed to organise form. It is only by applying a particular and suitable force that you can bring order and vitality and thence beauty into a plate of iron filings, which are otherwise as "ugly" as anything under heaven. The design in the magnetised iron filings expresses a confluence of energy. It is not "meaningless" or "inexpressive."

.   .   .   .

The vorticist is expressing his complex consciousness. He is not like the iron filings, expressing electrical magnetism; not like the automatist, expressing a state of cell-memory, a vegetable or

[6] For the denunciations, see *Blast, passim;* the quotation may be found in *Gaudier-Brzeska,* 90.

visceral energy. . . . One, as a human being, cannot pretend fully to express oneself unless one express instinct and intellect together. The softness and the ultimate failure of interest in automatic painting are caused by a complete lack of conscious intellect.[7]

In the "Medievalism" essay, he used the same emblem: "For the modern scientist energy has no borders, it is a shapeless 'mass' of force . . . . The rose that his magnet makes in the iron filings, does not lead him to think of the force in botanic terms, or wish to visualize that force as floral and extant *(ex stare)*." [8] Another repetition of the figure in *Guide to Kulchur* shows more clearly that he used it to symbolize survival or permanence, i.e., the power of "tradition":

The *forma*, the immortal *concetto*, the concept, the dynamic form which is like the rose pattern driven into the dead iron-filings by the magnet, not by material contact with the magnet itself, but separate from the magnet. Cut off by the layer of glass, the dust and filings rise and spring into order. Thus the *forma*, the concept rises from death
> The bust outlasts the throne
> The coin Tiberius.[9]

One analogy begets another: magnetism led Pound to make sculpture an analogue. The lines translated from Gautier at the end of the quoted passage (compressed from "L'Art") indicate the progression, and embody Gautier's precept that Pound paraphrased thus: "He exhorts us to cut in hard substance, the shell and the Parian. . . . to cut, metaphorically, in hard stone, etc." [10] Association between poetry and sculpture became so obsessive and implicatory in Pound's mind that it is possible to draw from

[7] "Affirmations: Vorticism," *New Age*, XVI (1915), 277, 278.
[8] *Literary Essays*, 154.
[9] *Guide to Kulchur*, 152.
[10] "The Hard and the Soft in French Poetry," *Poetry*, XI (1918), 265; *Literary Essays*, 285–86.

it conclusions even more wide-ranging than those reached by
Donald Davie in his *Ezra Pound: Poet as Sculptor*. Carved verse
meant for Pound something with a chance of lasting, something
that could add to the tradition; it meant something disciplined
and precise, demanding intense care, craftsmanship, and control; it meant something with hard surfaces, clear outlines,
"exact definition"; and it satisfied the peculiar craving of the
modernists for "spatial form." [11] In the present context it sums
up the eliciting of form by force: sculpture is that art most obviously and literally requiring great force to bring out form.
The other Vorticists, like Pound, insisted on the need to apply
the force of "will and consciousness"—a "complex consciousness" including instinct and racial memory—to draw forth the
expressive form in material. Gaudier-Brzeska, whose impact on
Pound was fateful, was particularly dogmatic about the "racial"
part of it: his "Vortex" statements are full of terms like "Paleo-
lithic vortex," "Hamitic vortex," "Semitic vortex." [12] Pound
listened raptly to the younger man's theories of sculpture and
culture; he began to find expanded significance in such practices as cutting directly in stone or metal without preliminary
models, an idea which Gaudier picked up from Jacob Epstein.
Gaudier generalized an aesthetic law from it: "No more arbitrary translations of a design in any material. . . . Epstein, whom
I consider the foremost in the small number of good sculptors in
Europe, lays particular stress on this." [13] Perhaps as much as anything else the motto "cut direct" crystallized Pound's determination never to impose external form on his material, but to apply

[11] The notion of "spatial form" was first treated, I believe, by Joseph
Frank in "Spatial Form in Modern Literature," first published in 1945 in
the *Sewanee Review*, and often reprinted since. The significance of this
idea is, however, only now being understood.
[12] See *Blast* No. 1, and No. 2 (July, 1915); *Gaudier-Brzeska*, 20–28;
Guide to Kulchur, 63–70.
[13] *Gaudier-Brzeska*, 31; cf. 76.

"forces" in order to reveal whatever was latent in it: the stone must "know" the form the carver imparts.

Pound's most complex statement on sculpture implies that he saw it as ideally an art of incarnation that could make immanent the transcendent powers of a "vital universe." By a "vortex" of concentration and force the sculptor can get into his stone something eternal:

> The best Egyptian sculpture is magnificent plastic, but its force comes from a non-plastic idea, i.e. the god is inside the statue.
> I am not considering the merits of the matter, much less those merits as seen by a modern aesthetic purist. I am using historic method. The god is inside the stone, *vacuos exercet aera morsus*. The force is arrested, but there is never any question about its latency, about the force being the essential, and the rest "accidental" in the philosophic technical sense. . . .
> This sculpture with something inside, revives in the Quattrocento portrait bust. But the antecedents are in verbal manifestation.[14]

Egyptian statues, unlike the Greek, are non-mimetic, not "caressable"; instead of reproducing the soft outlines of a human body, the stone manifests the hard outline of god-substance. Pound had somewhat overcautiously defined "a god" as "an eternal state of mind," but here the term is more concrete, epiphanic, and suggestive of the force "arrested" in the stone.[15] In another passage Pound underlined a continuity between carving gods in stones and the metamorphic tradition in general, implying that the Vorticist process was also one of incarnation. This passage is part of an attempt to answer the question "What have they done for me these vorticist artists?"

"I have not repulsed God in his manifestations," says the old

[14] "Medievalism" (see note 37 to Chap. Four); *Literary Essays*, 152–53.
[15] The definition came in "Religio, or the Child's Guide to Knowledge," published anonymously in the *New Freewoman*, I (1913), 173–74; reprinted in *Pavannes and Divisions*.

Egyptian poet. To-day I see so many who could not say, or who
could scarcely say it, for these manifestations at their intensest
are the manifestations of men in the heat of their art, of men
making instruments, for the best art is perhaps only the making
of instruments.

A clavicord or a statue or a poem, wrought out of ages of
knowledge, out of fine perception and skill, that some other
man, that a hundred other men, in moments of weariness can
wake beautiful sound with little effort, that they can be carried
out of the realm of annoyance into the calm realm of truth, into
the world unchanging, the world of fine animal life, the world
of pure form. And John Heydon. long before our present day
theorists, had written of the joys of pure form . . . inorganic,
geometrical form, in his "Holy Guide." [16]

In this passage Pound projected the Vorticist striving for "pure
form" into a penetration of the world of gods, "a world unchanging," with the implication that great works are not so
much ends in themselves as instrumentalities for such penetration. Great works are examples of the "bust thru from quotidien
into 'divine or permanent world.' " So the "magic moments" or
"moments of metamorphosis" in the *Cantos* present many gods,
many instruments. A work of art may achieve such a condition
if it is "wrought out of ages of knowledge," by a skill that is
the product of tradition. The "ages of knowledge," the tradition Pound refers to, is of course one that carries along the bits
of intense, direct "interpretation" of the "vital universe." In the
hands of a great craftsman these bits are fused together in a way
that makes them a vision of a god, or a myth—many sexual il-
luminations suddenly blazoning forth the figure of Aphrodite—
or, at a slightly lower voltage, into a contribution to a "morphology of experience." The best emblems of the process are
statues in which you can see the god in the stone, but as Pound
noted about the Quattrocento portrait busts, "the antecedents
are in verbal manifestation."

[16] *Gaudier-Brzeska*, 127.

Pound's obsession with the statue metaphor in part explains why he sometimes writes as if the art of poetry were a matter of chipping away detritus to reveal a progressively articulated image. He seems to see this not only as the individual poet's work but as the shape of the whole art: when he talks about his research into "what has been done, once for all," and into "what remains for us to do," his words evoke an image of gradual emergence, like that of the form in a late Michelangelo statue.[17] Erwin Panofsky tells us that "Michelangelo's figures are not conceived in relation to an organic axis but in relation to the surfaces of a rectangular block, the forms emerging from the stone as from the water in a slowly drained vessel. . . . They reveal the almost totemistic feeling of the natural-born stonecarver who refused the title of sculpture to any work produced *'per via di porre'* (modelling in clay or wax) instead of *'per forza di levare'* (cutting directly in the 'hard, alpine stone')." [18] Michelangelo's conception, and the Vorticist one as well, seem to rest on the ancient philosophic doctrine of potentiality, which tended to define "enduring essence" as a full manifestation, all of a thing that might emerge into being. Pound's thinking suggests a vision of endless and continuous articulation, an idea not disharmonious with Eliot's proposal in "Tradition and the Individual Talent" that each new "monument" modifies the existing order slightly.

The transcendental philosophic language employed here should not mislead us into thinking that "tradition" for these two poets was an academic exercise. Neither was it a ritual of recondite scholarship. The fervor of their preaching belies a

[17] As in "Prolegomena": "My pawing over the ancients and semi-ancients has been one struggle to find out what has been done, once for all, better than it can ever be done again, and to find out what remains for us to do, and plenty does remain. . . ." See *Literary Essays*, 11.

[18] Erwin Panofsky, *Studies in Iconology: Humanistic Themes in the Art of the Renaissance*, Torchbook ed. (New York and Evanston, 1962), 177–78.

merely snobbish purpose: they believed that they were engaged
in a real war, against forces of triviality, insularity, nihilism, and
catabolism. They feared that lack of "the historical sense" dis-
solved values and obscured definitions, and thought they saw
just this happening in the literary columns of current periodicals. Of course they tended to dramatize the cause; Eliot saw it
as a grim unheroic struggle.

> And what there is to conquer
> By strength or submission, has already been discovered
> Once or twice, or several times, by men whom one cannot hope
> To emulate—but there is no competition—
> There is only the fight to recover what has been lost
> And found and lost again and again: and now, under conditions
> That seem unpropitious.

The menace in the last phrase is underscored by the wartime
imagery—"raids," "squads," and so forth—that surrounds these
lines in *East Coker*. The imagery was natural enough in 1940,
but I think it owes something to the fact that the Vorticists had
dropped the nineteenth-century metaphor of revolution in favor
of war, and hence the struggle for tradition was often couched
in terms of a war. (Eliot was not a member of the Vorticist
group, but the first publication of his poems in England was in
their periodical *Blast*, and he did offer to write an essay on
Pound's Vorticist theory.)[19] Vorticist propaganda is full of the
metaphor: Pound called Wyndham Lewis "a man at war," and
declared that "the artist has at last been aroused to the fact that
the war between him and the public is a war without truce." All
this went on in the summer of 1914, and the first issue of *Blast*

[19] The offer, made to Harriet Monroe, is reported by Stanley K. Coffman, Jr., in his dissertation (see note 3 to Chap. Two), 92–93. The poems
published in *Blast* No. 2 were "Preludes" and "Rhapsody of [*sic*] a Windy
Night."

appeared only a few weeks before the First World War broke out. In the second issue Pound crowed: "While all other periodicals were whispering PEACE . . . 'BLAST' alone dared to present the actual discords of modern 'civilization,' DISCORDS now only too apparent in the open conflict between teutonic atavism and unsatisfactory democracy." [20] The Vorticists did not glorify war like the Futurists, since for them it was "only a symptom of the real disease," but they tended to identify themselves with the warlike state of mind.[21] Wyndham Lewis nominated himself, Pound, Eliot, and Joyce as "the men of 1914." Even in Pound's talk about "force" there is a bellicose, hostile note, perhaps a hint of the fatal lure of fascism. "It is only by applying a particular and suitable force that you can bring order and vitality and thence beauty into a plate of iron filings, which are otherwise as 'ugly' as anything under heaven." Tradition, like Imagist poetics in general, was conceived as a disciplinary idea, a force of "order" against the chaos of the struggles of our time, which must be fought

> With shabby equipment always deteriorating
> In the general mess of imprecision of feeling,
> Undisciplined squads of emotion.

The Dance of the Intellect Among Words

Among the effects on Pound's poetics of the alliance with Eliot was a broadening of perspectives. One augmentation stands out: a new tolerance of wordplay in the form of *logo-*

---

[20] *Blast* No. 2, 85–86. The earlier quotations are from "Wyndham Lewis," *Egoist,* I (1914), 233, and "The New Sculpture," *Egoist,* I (1914), 68.

[21] See *Letters,* 46–47: "This war is possibly a conflict between two forces almost equally detestable. Atavism and the loathsome spirit of mediocrity cloaked in graft. . . . One wonders if the war is only a stop gap. Only a symptom of the real disease."

poeia. This new interest is related to an awareness of Laforgue, whose interest for Pound went up sharply after he met Eliot. Among the joint activities conducted by these two, exploration of French poetry was one they accorded much importance; Gautier's influence on them is well known, and Laforgue's is perhaps even more important. Laforguian effects led Pound to see more possibilities in what he at first called "verbalism" than he had earlier acknowledged.

I do not think one can too carefully discriminate between Laforgue's tone and that of his contemporary French satirists. He is the finest wrought; he is most "verbalist." Bad verbalism is rhetoric, or the use of *cliché* unconsciously, or a mere playing with phrases. But there is good verbalism, distinct from lyricism or imagism, and in this Laforgue is a master. . . . Verbalism demands a set form used with irreproachable skill. Satire needs, usually, the form of cutting rhymes to drive it home.[22]

The last sentences make it clear that Laforgue was as important as Gautier in crystallizing the decision to go to "rhyme and regular strophes," the basic form of *Mauberley*. Apparently Pound and Eliot decided that the age demanded sharp-edged satire, and that clipped regular form, scored in the apparently "caressable" but really disturbing "sculpture" of rhyme, would draw the ridiculous poses of the age into cramped and uncomfortable display. A technique that could mock pretentious rhetoric was required; Pound named it *logopoeia*, dropping "verbalism," and defined it as

"The dance of the intellect among words," that is to say, it employs words not only for their direct meaning, but it takes count in a special way of habits of usage, of the context we *expect* to find with the word, its usual concomitants, of its known acceptances, and of ironical play. It holds the aesthetic content which is peculiarly the domain of verbal manifestation, and cannot

22 "Irony, Laforgue, and Some Satire," 97; *Literary Essays,* 283.

possibly be contained in plastic or in music. It is the latest come, and perhaps most tricky and undependable mode.[23]

It was certainly the latest come in his own poetics; to practice it meant bending the rules about stripping words of all association to get a precise meaning. Yet was it really discontinuous with Imagism? I think not. The presentation of complexes can be done by more than one technique, and the unsettling nuances of certain words in certain contexts themselves may form complexes. What the new technique really consisted of, as the works of both Pound and Eliot in this period amply illustrate, was the use of exact imprecisions, carefully designed indefinitions, just slightly inappropriate usages. To put it somewhat oversimply, Imagism as discipline had done its work; Pound now had such control of his style that he was able to turn old abhorrences like "suggestiveness" and "verbalism" against themselves. True, Pound differentiated *logopoeia* from *melopoeia* and *phanopoeia*, and this was roughly equivalent to his earlier separation of "verbalism" from "lyricism or imagism," quoted above. But I would suggest that the reduced meaning of "imagism" had to do with Pound's effort to disentangle himself from Amy Lowell's group, which went on calling itself "Imagist." Nowhere in the early writings does Pound define Imagism as narrowly as he did *phanopoeia*, as a "casting of images upon the visual imagination." In order to escape guilt by association, Pound did not want to call himself an "Imagist" any longer; hence he moved on to the tripartite poetics and the straitened definitions.[24]

In a sense, everything that is part of Pound's mature poetics

---

[23] "How to Read"; *Literary Essays*, 25.

[24] See *ABC of Reading*, 52: "I have taken to using the term phanopoeia to get away from irrelevant particular connotations tangled with a particular group of young people who were writing in 1912." Cf. *Letters*, 216: "Soi-disant 'imagists'—'bunch of goups' trop paresseux pour supporter sévérité de mes premiers 'Don'ts' et du clause 2me du manifest: 'Use no superfluous word.' "

was latent in the earlier conceptions of Imagism. The assured control that *logopoeia* demanded was immensely facilitated by the severities to which Pound faced up when practicing Imagism as discipline. He had trained himself; and he saw that Eliot had done the same thing. On meeting Eliot, Pound exclaimed: "He is the only American I know of who has made what I can call adequate preparation for writing. He has actually trained himself *and* modernized himself *on his own*."[25] The key word "modernized" suggests that Pound saw Eliot's self-discipline as not fundamentally dissimilar to his own. Further, in 1917 Pound evaluated Eliot's art in terms that imply that he viewed it as a mingling of techniques, some almost imagistic and others logopoeic:

> Were I a French critic, skilled in their elaborate art of writing books about books, I should probably go to some length discussing Mr. Eliot's two sorts of metaphor: his wholly unrealizable, always apt, half ironic suggestion, and his precise realizable picture. It would be possible to point out his method of conveying a whole situation and half a character by three words of a quoted phrase; his constant aliveness, his mingling of a very subtle observation with the unexpectedness of a back-handed cliché.[26]

Evidently Pound felt that there was no tension in such a mixture of modes. Moreover, if we examine Pound's work even in the Imagist period we find him using techniques very like Eliot's hybrids. Here is a sketch from a series called "Ladies" that neatly fits the last-named technique in the quoted passage:

> Four and forty lovers had Agathas in the old days,
> All of whom she refused;

[25] *Letters*, 40.
[26] "T. S. Eliot," 265; *Literary Essays*, 419. Basically, however, Pound saw Eliot as a supreme practitioner of *logopoeia:* see the Rome broadcast quoted by Norman in *Ezra Pound*, 381.

And now she turns to me seeking love,
And her hair also is turning.

Thus, while Pound owed to Eliot and Laforgue a new flexibility and a broadened sweep of perspective, he did not see that their lessons involved him in any self-contradictions. The enthusiastic practice of *logopoeia* on which he embarked implied for him no devaluation of earlier modes, only certain narrowed definitions for the sake of neatness and clarity. He triumphantly discovered *logopoeia* in Propertius, and made it part of his *Homage;* but he also discovered a "limited range" of it "in all satire," and "something like it" in Heine, who had been one of his earlier enthusiasms. Laforgue, he said, had "found or refound" the technique.[27]

The general effect of Laforgue on Pound seems to have been the opening up of new visions of continuities. Just as he saw new continuities in technique as a result of the Laforgue-Eliot impingement, so he saw a new relationship between composition and criticism in the Laforguian practice of *logopoeia.* "He is an incomparable artist. He is, nine-tenths of him, critic—dealing for the most part with literary poses and *clichés,* taking them as his subject matter. . . . He has done, sketchily and brilliantly, for French literature a work not incomparable to what Flaubert was doing for 'France' in *Bouvard and Pécuchet.*" [28] This insight into the real continuity between critical and creative activities led directly to the "Date Line" essay, where Pound affirmed his conviction that besides "criticism by discussion" there could be "criticism by translation," "criticism by exercise in the style of a given period," and finally "criticism in new com-

[27] "How to Read"; *Literary Essays,* 33. The only major fault of Warren Ramsay's perceptive essay on "Pound, Laforgue and Dramatic Structure," *Comparative Literature,* III (1951), 47–56, is the assumption that *logopoeia* necessitated some break with Imagism.
[28] "Irony, Laforgue, and Some Satire"; *Literary Essays,* 282–83.

position": "For example the criticism of Seneca in Mr. Eliot's
Agon is infinitely more alive, more vigorous than in his essay
on Seneca." [29] Bringing as it does not only poetry and criticism
but also translation into the continuum, this idea provided Pound
with a significant extension of his earlier belief in the interpenetration of poetry and scholarship, and it colors the purposes of
his art from about 1917 onwards. His poetry after that time
mixes poetic, translational, and critical activities with great freedom, just as it mixes the modes of *phanopoeia, melopoeia*, and
logopoeia.

Mauberley, as critics have long been pointing out, provides
an open field for logopoeic wordplay, with many varieties of
"just-wrong" usage, exact imprecision. Perhaps even more interesting are the further consequences of the new flexibility.
Mauberley's dominant technique seems to aim at the delineation
of a set of ominous vaguenesses in the British ambience; perhaps
Pound was going back to his statement of 1913 that "you can be
wholly precise in representing a vagueness." [30] Let us take Lady
Valentine for an example:

> Poetry, her border of ideas,
> The edge, uncertain, but a means of blending
> With other strata
> Where the lower and higher have ending;
>
> A hook to catch the Lady Jane's attention,
> A modulation toward the theatre,
> Also, in the case of revolution,
> A possible friend and comforter.

She wears the patronage of poetry like a garment, but can't
quite decide *which* garment. What is registered here is the emp-

[29] *Literary Essays*, 75.
[30] "The Serious Artist"; *Literary Essays*, 44.

tiness of twentieth-century British social attitudes, even the avowedly sympathetic, toward art. It is manifested in the inner uncertainty that all the Lady Valentines and Ottolines must have felt in assuming, presumptuously as they knew, the mantle of directress of the arts.

The latter sections of the poem make even more insistent use of the technique, especially in characterizing Mauberley's "drift."

> Amid the precipitation, down-float
> Of insubstantial manna,
> Lifting the faint susurrus
> Of his subjective hosanna.

This Biblical imagery, ironically recording Mauberley's "exodus" from the world of letters, yields no "realizable picture," but reveals a crucial inner blurring, an abdication of awareness. Such things are not less real for being vague, and the end was still registration of realities, with the basic means still that mastery of proportion between detail and insight that constitutes "presentation." We still find the skeletalizing, outlining tendency: "complexes," shapes of experience rendered in a few strokes, concentrated into a few lines:

> Charm, smiling at the good mouth,
> Quick eyes gone under earth's lid.

Again no picture, no "battle-scene," but an economical use of the potentialities of visual detail for instantaneous definition.

Another new flexibility that seems to be in some way contingent on the new freedom of wordplay shows itself in the development of *personae*. Patently *Mauberley* is in some sense a response to *Prufrock*, and the means by which Eliot conveyed Prufrock's indecisions may well have suggested techniques for

Pound. The analogy between the poems is almost too obvious. Pound alluded to it himself: "Of course, I'm no more Mauberley than Eliot is Prufrock." [31] As the remark indicates, the relationship of the poems turns on the question of *personae*. We know that the early work of Pound, and Eliot as well, shows heavy influence from Browning's dramatic monologues. That this should be so testifies not only to Browning's domination of the poetic landscape of their youth, but to the utility of these poems for their "scholarship": they point the way to an effort to "make the dead live." In 1918 Pound commented that "the most interesting form of modern poetry is to be found in Browning's 'Men and Women,'" and he added a curious afterthought: "From Ovid to Browning this sort of poem was very much neglected." [32] What he meant by that is explained in a passage from *The Spirit of Romance:* "Ovid, before Browning, raises the dead and dissects their mental processes; he walks with the people of myth." [33] So Pound's interest in Browning falls neatly into the perspective of the "Apostolic Succession," that early attempt to secure a "live tradition" by making the ghosts of the great dead drink blood. His fascination with dramatic monologues was therefore due not so much to their enshrining a "poetry of experience" as to their raising of these ghosts: Browning, for Pound, presents a Victorian version of a "poetry of incarnation."

But Browning's attempts to catch back history were only useful up to a point. In Pound's career there is a progression from Browningesque dramatic monologues to less characterological studies in the form. Compare "Sestina: Altaforte," where there is an interest in "character" that Browning would have relished —and Strindberg deplored—with the puzzles of "Near Perigord,"

[31] *Letters*, 180.
[32] "Chinese Poetry II," *To-day*, III (1918), 93.
[33] *The Spirit of Romance*, 16.

and then go on to that study of a "mere surface," *Hugh Selwyn Mauberley*. (Something similar goes from *Prufrock* to the shifting voices of *The Waste Land*, but Eliot began at a different point.) The earliest monologues were conceived as soliloquies, as Pound explained in 1908:

To me the short so-called dramatic lyric—at any rate the sort of thing I do—is the poetic part of a drama the rest of which (to me the prose part) is left to the reader's imagination or implied or set in a short note. I catch the character I happen to be interested in at the moment he interests me, usually a moment of song, self-analysis, or sudden understanding or revelation. And the rest of the play would bore me and presumably the reader. I paint my man as I *conceive* him.[34]

But as his poetics matured he abandoned the "fragment of a drama" approach. His acquisition of a taste for thinned-out, skeletal *personae* runs parallel to the growth of his distaste for drama: in 1916 he grumbled that "drama is a dam'd form, tending nearly always toward work of secondary intensity," and in later years he grew even more intolerant: "I think the reason I loathe all stage stuff is that it is split . . . . Anything that asks the reader to think of effect or how it wd. be on stage distracts from reality of fact presented. Even if it does appeal to the ballet russe or charlotte russe instincts of the beeholder. Means the author not obsessed with reality of his subject." [35] This passage is an important one; for one thing, it demonstrates how obsessive was Pound's insistence on a "poetry of reality." But for the present purpose, it serves to indicate that the demands of "reality of fact presented" were so uncompromising as to rule out any kind of dramatic illusion such as "character." A determinative distinction must be made at this point: a *persona* is not necessarily a character. Of course the two may be telescoped, and often are

34 *Letters*, 3–4.
35 *Letters*, 81 and 306.

by Browning—but not very often by Pound or Eliot. A. C. Bradley's kind of Shakespearean criticism, speculating on the "real lives" of the *dramatis personae,* could be applied to many of Browning's poems, but has proved incompetent to deal with Prufrock.[36] By 1914 Pound made it clear, in the passage already quoted (p. 130), that he had not really been much interested in character anyhow, and that his *personae* were really "masks of the self," seeming verities in the "search for oneself." This fact further suggests the simple truth that the speaker in a Pound poem, no matter what mask he wears, is always Pound himself. Not that he was interested in self-revelation or self-projection in the ultra-Romantic sense: rather, his method commits him so intensely to "what is being presented" that he could spend no more time on "building a character" than on novelistic accretion of detail. *Logopoeia* suits such an attitude perfectly, since it places the locus of interest in the speaker's words, but not for the sake of "dramatic decorum" implying the "character" of the speaker. It makes us think rather of what ironic possibilities the words would have if viewed in shifting or flexible perspectives; it makes us less interested in having a thorough understanding of the speaker's character than in grasping all that the words might mean uttered by various speakers. It makes us desire flexible *personae,* as characterless as possible, in short "mere surfaces" like Mauberley.[37]

As early as the "Contemporania" poems Pound was beginning to experiment with various ways of using himself as a *persona.* Sometimes this took the form of putting himself into the poem directly as one of the *dramatis personae;* sometimes it meant

[36] For an interesting discussion of the inadequacy of this kind of reading, see C. K. Stead, *The New Poetic: Yeats to Eliot* (New York, 1966), 148–55. Stead's analysis confirmed my own view that a *persona* is not a character.

[37] Pound so describes Mauberley in a 1922 letter to his old teacher, Felix Schelling: see *Letters,* 180.

constructing an unnamed *persona* as the speaker of the poem who appears to be the poet but actually is not—like Byron's device in *Don Juan*. The new flexibility of *personae* in the "*logopoeia* phase" of his poetics seems to have led him to further experiments, extending and combining various devices. One result that is interesting as a preliminary study for *Mauberley* is the poem "Villanelle: The Psychological Hour." In it Pound treats urbanely a state of mind he once put in these terms: "Any man whose youth has been worth anything, any man who has lived his life at all in the sun, knows that he has seen the best of it when he finds thirty approaching." [38] For "Villanelle" Pound adopts the mask of a middle-aging aesthete repelled by crudeness around him, fearful of his life and his friends leaving him, and of frightening off new friends by overmuch posing. He sings a refrain: "Beauty is so rare a thing./ So few drink of my fountain." As he awaits a hoped-for visit from a new couple (with a hint of desperation in "Friends? Are people less friends/ because one has just, at last, found them?") he wonders did he "talk like a fool,/ The first night?/ The second evening?" The poem ends:

> Now the third day is here—
>   no word from either;
> No word from her nor him,
> Only another man's note:
>   "Dear Pound, I am leaving England."

Calling the middle-aging aesthete by his own name was a good joke here, involving the kind of self-mockery that Eliot and Joyce occasionally used to brilliant effect; but for a larger work, "an attempt to condense the James novel," Pound decided on a different strategy, which was to create a fading aesthete named Hugh Selwyn Mauberley.

[38] *Gaudier-Brzeska,* 45–46.

The problem that stymies so many commentators on this poem is precisely that of fully understanding that Mauberley is *not* a character, that by this time there was nothing left for Pound in the "fragment of a drama" approach. Donald Davie, for instance, ruins some good perceptions by trying to impose demands suitable for closet drama, and gets more and more annoyed when he cannot figure out just who is speaking: "We have to say that the whole first sequence of twelve short poems reads better, that several difficulties are ironed out, if they are taken as spoken by the fictional Mauberley. Yet many of them can be read as if spoken directly by Pound." [39] Indeed they are all spoken by Pound, who holds up various masks which are not so much identities as accents or tones of voice. The *personae* of this section are as shifting as the speakers in *The Waste Land,* and there are violent shifts of viewpoint, e.g., between the first and second short poems. The unity is one of subject: the causes of Mauberley's decline into oblivion. The first poem gives the version of the British world of letters; later speakers have some things to say about that world, indicting it as typical of a society that could indulge in a murderous squabble like the First World War on the pretext that it was defending culture, which in truth meant nothing more to it than "two gross of broken statues" or "a few thousand battered books." In this vein the speakers remind us that England had managed to suppress or ignore its most dedicated artists in one generation after another. Since Mauberley, beyond his function as subject, is but a series of momentary inflections, it is not worthwhile trying to state just where his "voice" is heard. Pound was obsessed with the reality of his subject, not with portraiture. If we listen sensitively, and with an ear attuned to logopoeic possibilities, we shall perhaps find that the speakers of the moment are sufficiently defined by what

[39] "Ezra Pound's *Hugh Selwyn Mauberley,*" in *The Modern Age: Volume* 7 *of the Pelican Guide to English Literature* (Baltimore, 1963), 323.

they say, and that occasional phrases that might be taken several ways are deliberately so designed. In many places the effect depends on our seeing "layers" of context—different accents *within* a given phrase. Hugh Kenner points out, for instance, that the line "His true Penelope was Flaubert" has an ironic truth for Pound invisible to the "uncomprehending but not unsympathetic" speaker who says it:

For Pound, Flaubert is the true (=faithful) counterpart, entangling crowds of suitors (superficial "realists") in their own self-deceit while she awaits the dedicated partner whose arm can bend the hard bow of the "mot juste". . . . For the writer of the epitaph, on the other hand, Flaubert is conceded to be E. P.'s "true" (=equivalent) Penelope only in deprecation: Flaubert being for the English literary mind of the first quarter of the present century a foreign, feminine, rather comically earnest indulger in quite un-British preciosity.[40]

Other phrases throughout the poem have similarly shifting or flexible values: if we take "Attic grace" or "the classics in paraphrase" to mean Gilbert Murray's Aeschylus or the Lang, Leaf, Butcher, and Myers Homer, then we get exactly the reading we deserve—a fatuous one. This is perhaps an unfriendly device, but entirely probable given Pound's state of mind. So also if we take "the relation of the state to the individual" of the later sections in a Fabian sense. Probably the finest example is "conservation of the 'better tradition.' " Those questionable quotation marks, the blandness of the utterance, the dignified rhyme and the ballet of words ending in "-ation"—all will subtly mislead us if we forget Pound's war against those whose idea of the "better tradition" was Milton, the Romantics, and the more "public-minded" Victorians.

True, some red herrings have obscured this simple reading, notably the "E. P." in the title of the first poem, and Pound's

[40] Kenner, *The Poetry of Ezra Pound*, 170–71.

later comment that "Mauberley buried E. P. in the first poem; gets rid of all his troublesome energies." [41] These have led some critics to conclude that the first poem is Mauberley's judgment of Pound. But what about phrases like "his true Penelope was Flaubert," and "the age demanded" from the second poem, which are emphatically applied not to Pound but to Mauberley in the second sequence of poems? What about the notation that the subject of the first poem is said to have striven to maintain "the sublime" (another equivocal phrase) "for three years," while Mauberley in the latter sequence "drank ambrosia" for three years? Is there not a suggestion that these refer to the same events? The latter part of the poem states that it presents Mauberley "under a more tolerant, perhaps, examination." More tolerant than what, if not the first poem? In this light the title "E. P. Ode Pour L'Election de Son Sepulchre" is simply an inside joke on Pound's need to excise parts of himself in order to arrive at the *persona* of the enervated Mauberley. For Mauberley is made, in part, of Pound's own "life and contacts" but with the liveliest elements suppressed, or buried: he is what Pound might have become without those "troublesome energies."

Davie's view issues in this judgment: "Hardly anything is lost, and much is gained, if the poems are read one at a time, as so many poems by Pound, and if the Mauberley persona is dismissed as a distracting nuisance. *Hugh Selwyn Mauberley* thus falls to pieces, though the pieces are brilliant, intelligent always, and sometimes moving." [42] This is seeing and not seeing; Mauberley is a nuisance only if you try to make him more than he is. The same assumption is at work here that can make a real botch of reading *The Waste Land*, that the poem is a fragmentary drama with names of speakers unfortunately blotted out. Pound is the speaker in his poems, as Davie sees but cannot comprehend;

[41] Quoted from a personal letter by Thomas E. Connolly, "Further Notes on Mauberley," *Accent*, XVI (1956), 59.
[42] Davie, *Ezra Pound: Poet as Sculptor*, 101.

the distinctions between the various angles he speaks from are not important save as indicated in the lines themselves, by what Pound called in the *Cantos* "various colourings and degrees of importance or emphasis attributed by the protagonist of the moment." [43] Mauberley himself remains a "mere surface," and no one should be interested in his life outside the borders of the poem. The art of the poem is certainly not in Mauberley's depth of character, for he was never meant to have any; it is rather in the oblique Jamesian method of conveying a series of events through "reflectors." In fact, the subtlest character in the poem is the judicious *persona* of the latter part, who analyzes the "isolation/ Which these presents place/ Under a more tolerant, perhaps, examination." (Just the right flavor of Prayer Book and law court is given by "these presents.")

If Mauberley himself has any interest beyond his superficial resemblance to Pound, or to the *persona* in "Villanelle," it may be in his reflection of some parts of the life of Ford Madox Hueffer—who bears an equally sonorous tripartite name. Kenner long ago noted that the tenth poem of the first sequence suggests "the post-war fortunes of Ford Madox Ford," who "on his discharge from the army retired in disgust to Sussex to raise pigs." [44] In fact he was continually "retiring" from literary life. For Pound he was "the stylist" who was pre-eminently "unpaid, uncelebrated," and he did offer "succulent cooking," that being one of his hobbies—though his mistresses were anything but "placid and uneducated." He had suffered the "hysterias, trench confessions,/ laughter out of dead bellies" firsthand. Moreover, Pound seems to have seen his postwar period of "drift" in terms that sometimes suggest Mauberley's failures. It is again Kenner who points out that one of Mauberley's symptoms is shown in his "insisting on visual analogies in the presence of auditory fact," as he cultivates his art of medallions: such an art can only

[43] *Letters*, 322.
[44] Kenner, *The Poetry of Ezra Pound*, 174.

produce "a static homage, a *collage* of optical analogies." [45]
Compare Pound's remarks in 1923: "I think Hueffer goes wrong
because he bases his criticism on the eye, and almost solely on
the eye. Nearly everything he says applies to things *seen*. It is
the exact rendering of the visible image, the cabbage field *seen*,
France *seen* from the cliffs." [46] The connection with Mauberley's case is slight, but suggestive. Pound went on to insist that
there were other "pressures" to be made use of in art; staying
within one modality for him amounted to self-imprisonment—
which might lead, perhaps, to Mauberley's "anaesthesis." Inci-
dentally, this passage casts light on the relation of visualization
to Imagism: obviously Pound admired the clarity that Hueffer
achieved by "exact rendering of the visible image," but as the
lack of a visualization requirement in his early definitions shows,
he never had any intention of restricting himself to one means
toward clarity. The only "Imagist" theory that required visualization was Hulme's, and that of a sort greatly different from
the Hueffer-Pound clarity; Hulme wanted a "plaster model of a
thing to express [the poet's] emotion at the sight of the vision he
sees, his wonder and ecstasy." [47] (Cf. "a mould in plaster," Poem
II of *Mauberley*.)

In any case, however, the focus of the poem was not on personalities, but on the ignoble and maddening imperceptivity of
postwar London: Pound and Hueffer were driven away, and
Eliot into a sanatorium, in those years. The times must have
seemed to be bringing on a repetition of the treatment accorded
to artists recalled in *Mauberley*: the "English Rubaiyat," the
Pre-Raphaelites, Aesthetics, and men of the "Nineties" had suffered the same fate in rapid succession. This process was the
reality, this the object on which Pound kept his poet's eye fixed.

[45] Kenner, "Leucothea's Bikini: Mimetic Homage," in *Ezra Pound: Perspectives*, 38.
[46] "On Criticism in General," *Criterion*, I (1923), 146.
[47] *Further Speculations* (see note 12 to Chap. Two), 78.

SIX

FURTHER PERSPECTIVES

The Puritan Motive,
or Imagism as American Revolution

A CASE OUGHT to be made for the assertion that most metaphysical beliefs, and many cultural and literary ones, are at bottom displaced or disguised religious ideas. There can be little profit in continuing the underestimation of religious motives in an era when the tendency of the Protestant Ethic to spread into many areas of life has been so thoroughly demonstrated. It may be that one day we shall decide that Max Müller was wiser than he knew when he contended that the history of religions is the history of man. At all events the most philosophic kinds of ideas often seem to be held with a suspiciously mystical faith, or defended with prophetic fervor. Modernist thought is no exception. In some ways literary and religious thought are as intertwined in the twentieth century as they were in the seventeenth; to start with a demonstrable example, the influence of late nineteenth-century speculations in comparative religion and religious anthropology on the modern writers has long been plainly evident—so long indeed that it has become unfashionable to talk about it, and we are now told *not* to read *The Golden*

173

Bough and *From Ritual to Romance* to aid our studies of *The Waste Land*. But the relationship is as valid as ever, though it is of course much more devious than Eliot's footnotes imply.[1]

I have already used several ideas and metaphors drawn from religion in an attempt to clarify my analysis of Pound's thought. I meant these to be more than merely illustrative. Though at first Pound seems much less concerned with religious ideas than his friends Yeats, Eliot, and Joyce, their place in his mind is quite central, and they are crucial not only to his beliefs about mythology but, for example, to the whole conception of Imagist discipline. Most of the ideas I have used so far could roughly be characterized as Catholic ones, and the main point of the comparison is fairly simple: it can be seen in the Catholic insistence on the real and literal, not "symbolic," nature of what it deals with. Pound's belief in a "poetry of reality" starts from similar convictions. "The Image is not a substitute; it does not stand for anything but itself. . . . For [Imagists] the bread and wine are the body and the blood," as May Sinclair put it. In this connection it is interesting to note Pound's remark that "the Catholic Church went out of business when its hierarchy ceased to believe its own dogma." [2] Perhaps more than other modern poets Pound believes in the literal reality of what poems say; he was so irritated by the bourgeois equation of poetry with fantasy that his attack on it has been in a profound sense his life's work. Scornfully thinking of the world in which " 'Poetry! ! ! ' is used as a synonym for 'Bosh! Rott! ! Rubbish! ! ! ' " or identified with " 'lofty and flowery language,' " he wrote in 1911 that

[1] It is impossible to believe that the developments in the theories of myth and religion which were stimulated in those years, by scholars or charlatans, had no effect on modern literature. Neither the "Cambridge anthropologists" nor even Madame Blavatsky have been studied carefully enough in this regard, doubtless because generalities about their roles did in fact obscure other pertinent kinds of reading of the modern authors. I predict, however, that we will find ways to avoid the obscuring.

[2] *Guide to Kulchur,* 75.

"it is certain that the present chaos will endure until the Art of poetry has been preached down the amateur gullet, until there is such a general understanding of the fact that poetry is an art and not a pastime"; and nothing could madden him like "the old lie. . . . that poetry is made to entertain." [3] Pound's belief will seem naïve and literal-minded to skeptical analysts, and in that way as in others is related to orthodoxies that have long puzzled non-Catholics, such as Incarnation, transubstantiation, and the typological doctrine of the literal truth of the Old Testament. These examples should not be allowed to lead to the conclusion that only certain ineffable beliefs are in question: what Pound shares with Catholicism is not a love of mystery or a taste for paradox, but something more general having to do with an unusual need for treating "realities." Imagist registrations, Fenollosa's objective predications, and all the rest of the components of his poetics are important to him for just this reason.

The common assumptions are in fact better demonstrated by a more circuitous chain of associations. To put it briefly, there is a tenuous but unmistakable connection between the generally reactionary social thought of the great modernists and the social doctrines of some modern intellectual Catholics. It is not merely a matter of the influence of men like Maurras and Benda; there is a real affinity here, involving strenuous assertions of the "objective" reality of the external world. Apparently the animus of this thought is directed against a relativistic, skeptical subjectivism, somewhat too easily identified with liberal-democratic humanism, which is thought to undercut principles of authority and weaken moral fiber. The reasoning goes that if we can assert objective reality firmly enough, we shall have a basis from which to deduce comfortingly absolute moral laws. These are predictably found to coincide with the teachings of the Church.

[3] *Literary Essays*, 49, 29, 10, 64.

Why should men love the Church? Why should they love her
laws?
She tells them of Life and Death, and of all that they would
forget.
She is tender where they would be hard, and hard where they
like to be soft.
She tells them of Evil and Sin, and other unpleasant facts.
They constantly try to escape
From the darkness outside and within
By dreaming of systems so perfect that no one will need to be
good.[4]

Eliot writes of a Catholic Church that isn't exactly the Roman
one, but the difference is unimportant here. The ax ground in
these lines is that the Church deals with facts, whereas thoughts
of improving the social order are mere pipe dreams.

One version of this gospel was a recent semi-popular reduction of its economic principles into something called "Objectiv-
ism," led by the novelist Ayn Rand, which was meant to reassert
the saving power of capitalism. It is noteworthy that expositions
of this philosophy by Miss Rand or her followers usually began
with some form of the proposition that the external world actually and objectively exists. The inordinate emphasis on this proposition in all varieties of this thought reflects in an obscure way
the profounder strivings of the "poets of reality," and the affinity is part of the explanation of why the modernists tended to
be reactionary in politics. Even when like Joyce they began as
socialists, the progression was usually in a right-wing direction,
and few had any patience with the political processes of the
modern democracies.[5]

---

[4] T. S. Eliot, *The Complete Poems and Plays 1909–1950* (New York,
1952), 106; from "Choruses from 'The Rock.'"
[5] The number of marching songs written by them for fascist groups
was something of a scandal. But beyond such things I would point to the
career of Auden as illustrative of the almost irresistible momentum toward
the right.

As it happens, there are many specific causes for Pound's political and economic beliefs that have little to do with the pattern discernible here: pre-eminent among these was his conviction that munitions makers had prolonged World War I. Nonetheless, he is typically modernist in the directions toward which such convictions led him. The end result in his case was an extremist economic scheme, but if he had been as clerical as Eliot his authoritarian leanings might have taken a more traditional direction. He did go so far as to say in the *Guide to Kulchur* that "given a free hand with the Saints and Fathers one could construct a decent philosophy, not merely a philosophism. . . . you cd. erect inside the fabric something modern man cd. believe." Further on he said, "again I repeat: I cd. be quite a 'good catholic' IF they wd. let me pick my own saints and theologians." [6] We may take such statements as seriously as we choose.

Some literary men seem to be attracted toward Catholicism— though usually not so far as to commitment—in reaction against Protestant training or environment in youth: Byron is an example. This may well have been Pound's case too; certainly early Protestant training, and the diffused Puritan heritage of most Americans, show up in his ideas and his career, and form a pattern that is even more significant than his sympathies for Catholicism. The fervor, urgency, and absoluteness with which he delivered his opinions testifies to his origin from a country that takes evangelism seriously, and throughout his thought, from aesthetics to economics, something that looks suspiciously like a Puritan pattern keeps revealing itself. Imagist poetics is a useful example: it was founded on the idea of discipline, an *askesis* necessary for poetic purity. The Imagists sought no elusive *poésie pure*, of course, but they did demand a poetry purified of signs of decadence like rhetoric, comment, metronomic rhythm, "emotional slither," "Tennysonianness of speech," and many other immoral practices. Most puritanically they eschewed dec-

[6] *Guide to Kulchur*, 76 and 189.

oration and ornament, that Victorian gingerbread that obscures truth. Pound hunted the "decorative frill adjective" and its equivalents, in the writings of friends and strangers, with the zeal of a Salem judge. He ripped off a letter to Harriet Monroe on reading a certain lady's translation of Catullus in a 1916 number of *Poetry:* "LESBIAD. NO. HELL NO. . . . The most hard edged and intense of the Latin poets should *not* be cluttered with wedding-cake cupids and clichés like 'dregs of pain,' etc., etc., ad. inf. Pink blue baby ribbon." [7] He was equally severe on decorative form, denouncing superfluity and insisting, like Louis Sullivan or Frank Lloyd Wright, that form follow function. At many crucial places in his poetics Pound showed his native American respect for function, once defining great art as "maximum efficiency of expression." The corollary to this axiom is that nonfunctional matter is not only extraneous but somehow sinful and corrupting. It is in this sense that Imagism represents the American Revolution in poetry—more specifically, the American Puritan revolution. Pound described himself as having "a plymouth-rock conscience landed on predilection for the arts." [8]

The Puritanism can be seen in the ends as well as the means of Imagist technique. Hugh Kenner speaks contemptuously of those readers who ignore Pound because his "poetry of the surface" leaves them "panting for their emotional marching orders": "Many readers dismiss Pound's verse as cold and uninteresting. A trip to his zoo or his treasure-house doesn't send 'em. They yearn for the belly-punch." [9] With more sympathy (for the readers) Graham Hough laments Pound's fanatic suppression of emotional reverberation, which he ascribes to "a

[7] *Letters,* 69.

[8] *Ibid.,* 12. Note that Pound's sculptural metaphor for poetry was a purifying one: "Take a chisel and cut away all the stone you don't want" (*Letters,* 91).

[9] Kenner, *The Poetry of Ezra Pound,* 18, 73, 69–70.

defiant insistence on the surface of things, and an insistence that the surface of things is all." [10] As a matter of criticism in general, it is hard to decide whether Pound's restraint was too severe. Poetry is that art perhaps most liable to confusions between emotions described and emotions induced, and the optimum relation between poetry and feeling has not been demonstrated to the satisfaction of all. Pound was evidently determined, in any case, never to hand over emotions on a platter; above all, he abhorred a poetry infected with "luxurious riot." The effect was that his practice was uncompromisingly anti-hedonistic. This suited his Vorticist determination to "save the public's soul by punching its face," never to give "*homo canis*" anything he can glut on. Following Gaudier–Brzeska's lead Pound attacked "caressable" sculpture, such as Greek statues of the late periods, in which the viewer loves to fantasize himself. In his own art he reserved his most scathing contempt for those pleasurabilities that are self-indulgent by-products of reading or writing poetry: "It is only in the flurry, the shallow frothy excitement of writing, or the inebriety of a metre, that one falls into the easy—oh, how easy!—speech of books and poems that one has read." [11] Few poets would consider these pleasures very threatening, but Pound puritanically treats them as loathesomely infectious.

Not that Puritanism, in Pound's case or generally, can be very deeply understood by equating it with pleasure-hating as such —Pound like Coleridge proposed pleasure as the ultimate end of poetry. But he insisted that the reader must work to get it, and not read simply to gratify his tastes. The true pleasure cannot be obtained by simply demanding it, but comes with hard-earned understanding that requires self-mastery to achieve. Here Pound might well have agreed with I. A. Richards: "To read a poem

[10] Graham Hough, *Image and Experience*, 13.
[11] *Letters*, 49.

for the sake of the pleasure which will ensue if it is successfully read is to approach it in an inadequate attitude. Obviously it is the poem in which we should be interested, not in a by-product of having managed successfully to read it." [12] The Puritan feels he must guard against inadequacy not only in himself but in others. He has a Calvinist suspicion of corruptibility, and fears that man's appetites and anxieties leave him easy prey for "the inferior product ready for instant consumption." Naturally such an assumption can irritate readers; many have been heartily offended by Pound's desire to save their souls, and find little but cant in the *Cantos*. If their judgment is unfair they may at least be right in discerning the source of Pound's attitude in the didactic preachiness of Dissenting evangelism.

Pound himself ascribed his moral strenuousness to his belief that it is the duty of art to present reality. "I am perhaps didactic," he conceded. "It's all rubbish to pretend that art isn't didactic. A revelation is always didactic." Didacticism for Pound included preventing the reader from indulging his innately depraved taste for plot, story, and other mere "literary values," from which poetry should be purified; it included facing up to, even welcoming, the attacks which the angry reader inflicts on those who unsettle him with revelations of truth: the average man, Pound seems to have believed, "becomes not only a detester but a persecutor of living and unfolding ideas. He not only refuses them, but he wishes to prevent you from having them." Puritans thrive on persecution, and poets, being entrusted with a transcendent medium for recording revelations, must always be willing to risk suffering in the cause of truth. "If the poets don't make certain horrors appear horrible who will? All values ultimately come from our judicial sentences. (This arrogance is not mine but Shelley's, and it is absolutely true. Humanity is

12 I. A. Richards, *Principles of Literary Criticism*, Harvest ed. (New York, n.d.), 96–97.

malleable mud, and the arts set the moulds it is later cast into. Until the cells of humanity recognize certain things as excrement, they will stay in [the] human colon and poison it.)" [13] Nobody likes to be told he is malleable mud. Pound could have made the same point by saying something like "modes of human behavior show an almost infinite adaptability, and the arts form a very persuasive force for shaping them," but that might have smacked of flattering human nature, which the Puritan avoids at all costs.

The Puritan tradition entails the assumption that truth is not an elusive gleam behind the opacities of the universe, but simple and obvious, only obscured by human corruptibility and malevolence. Radical thought in America, being heavily Puritanized, frequently stands on this assumption.

Let us settle ourselves, and work and wedge our feet downward through the mud and slush of opinion, and prejudice, and tradition, and delusion, and appearance, that alluvion which covers the globe, through Paris and London, through New York and Boston and Concord, through Church and State, through poetry and philosophy and religion, till we come to a hard bottom and rocks in place, which we can call *reality*, and say, This is, and no mistake; and then begin, having a *point d'appui*, below freshet and frost and fire, a place where you might found a wall or a state, or set a lamp-post safely, or perhaps a gauge, not a Nilometer, but a Realometer, that future ages might know how deep a freshet of shams and appearances had gathered from time to time.[14]

That is Thoreau, but the idea is a logical extension of some themes of Puritan rhetoric. All we have to do to reach reality is to go back upstream to a purer flow, uncontaminated by silt. The assumption that truth is obscured only by men shows clearly in Pound's economic theories, which he called "perfectly

[13] *Letters*, 180, 181; *Gaudier-Brzeska*, 108.
[14] *Walden*, "Where I Lived and What I Lived For."

simple facts." Eliot very shrewdly remarked that Pound wrote
on economics as if his readers knew all that he had to say but had
failed to understand it—or, he might have added, had deliberately suppressed it.[15] The Puritanic prophet relishes inflicting his
message on those who have ears but hear not. He views the gen-
erations of men as such non-hearers; he may construct his own
"tradition," the accumulated wisdom of the ages, but suspects
that widely held "traditions" only preserve layers of sham and
appearance. For him no reverence is due a belief because many
have held it, just the opposite in fact: the more it has become
part of established institutions, the more suspect it tends to be.
For him the past is a floodplain of compounded errors, plus a
certain residue of prophetic visions. It must be endlessly filtered
to obtain truth.

Since the causes of error are certain spiritual diseases afflicting
men, the prophet develops a sharp eye for corruptions and infec-
tions. "I can tell the bank-rate and component of tolerance for
usury in any epoch by the quality of *line* in painting. Baroque,
etc., era of usury becoming tolerated." [16] Pound's moralist aesthetic is related to Ruskin's, but cares little for the "well-made"
or for guild-craft ethics. It is rather a puritanical smelling-
out of insidious, impersonal corruption. Throughout his career
Pound has been given to scientistic metaphors, many of which
show the same heightened awareness of infectibility. "It is as
important for the purpose of thought to keep language efficient
as it is in surgery to keep tetanus bacilli out of one's bandages";
or, "the disease of the last century and a half has been 'abstraction.' This has spread like tuberculosis." [17] Pound thunders

---

[15] T. S. Eliot, "Ezra Pound," *Poetry,* LXVIII (1946), 335. The essay has
been reprinted in *An Examination of Ezra Pound,* ed. Peter Russell (Norfolk, Conn., 1950) and in the Twentieth Century Views volume, *Ezra
Pound: A Collection of Critical Essays,* ed. Walter Sutton (Englewood
Cliffs, N.J., 1963).

[16] *Letters,* 303.

[17] *Literary Essays,* 22 and 59.

against the spread of rot wherever he sees it, and all the better if he finds it in centers of power. The Leveller side of Puritanism misread the Biblical denunciations of "evil in high places," which simply referred to backsliding Jews sacrificing in Canaanite mountaintop sanctuaries, as a warrant for morbid suspicion of the morals of kings and magistrates. Everyone in America knows the results, which range from parlor cynicism about "politics" and "graft" to genuine conspiracy theories, left or right wing. Pound's suspicions about international financiers and other shady repressive forces predictably developed into 1941 conclusions of "treason in the White House." That a number of Republicans reached similar conclusions does not excuse Pound, but stresses his typicality. The joy of the American in "exposés" of his leaders easily gets out of hand, and leads to seeing taints of corruption everywhere.

It may even be that Pound's abhorrence of "rhetoric" and "comment" owes more in the end to the ancient Biblical hostility toward sophistic eloquence than it does to Flaubert. Certainly many of Pound's statements on the problem suggest denunciations of those who make the worse appear the better reason. "An imperfect broken statement if uttered in sincerity often tells more to the auditor than the most meticulous caution of utterance could," he asserted, and elsewhere concluded that he had "ultimately a greater trust in rough speech than in eloquence." [18] Of the Renaissance Pound wrote: "Italy went to rot, destroyed by rhetoric, destroyed by the periodic sentence and by the flowing paragraph, as the Roman Empire had been destroyed before her. . . . They desired orators." [19] This mistrust of eloquence has figured in many controversies in literary history; in our time it seems to have played a part even in the

[18] *Guide to Kulchur*, 129 and 181. St. Augustine aptly quotes Cicero in expressing the Christian mistrust of eloquence. See *On Christian Doctrine* (note 19, Chap. Three), 121.
[19] *Gaudier-Brzeska*, 113–14.

eventual devaluation of conceptual thought and language, put in these terms by Ernst Cassirer:

If language is to grow into a vehicle of thought, an expression of concepts and judgments, this evolution can be achieved only at the price of forgoing the wealth and fullness of immediate experience. In the end, what is left of the concrete sense and feeling content it once possessed is little more than a bare skeleton. But there is one intellectual realm in which the word not only preserves its original creative power, but is ever renewing it; in which it undergoes a sort of constant palingenesis, at once a sensuous and a spiritual reincarnation. This regeneration is achieved as language becomes an avenue of artistic expression. Here it recovers the fullness of life.[20]

But this is a passionless statement of an attitude that was held by the modernists with much passion. What accounts for the vigor of poets' attacks on abstract thought? In part, perhaps, it was a vague but growing sense of the inadequacy of the metaphysical concepts that had dominated Western philosophy since the seventeenth century—a feeling that Whitehead later made explicit, that the system was full of "high abstractions" given a "misplaced concreteness." [21] And of course there were a multitude of other causes reinforcing their mistrust of conceptual discourse. But surely among these must have been the Biblical fear of sophistry, particularly sophistries used by the powerful for self-justification. The Puritans, following Ramistic hints, revived such fears against glib Establishmentarian persuasions. Sometimes Pound too seems to have thought that it was his mission to attack "abstraction" as the tool of "the old gang," the "liars in public places"—the Establishment in short.

The moralism that has inhered in Western literature since Plato's time, powerfully reinforced when the study of poetry

[20] Ernst Cassirer, *Language and Myth* (New York, 1946), 98.
[21] Alfred North Whitehead, *Science and the Modern World* (New York, 1926), 71–84, *et passim*.

became intertwined with training for the interpretation of Scripture, grew more complicated but not less pervasive when the Dissenting stream got thoroughly into the flow. When Wordsworth proposed to purify the "depraved taste" of a nation that had acquired a "degrading thirst after outrageous stimulation," and had become addicted to "frantic novels, sickly and stupid German Tragedies, and deluges of idle and extravagant stories in verse," he was making use of a moralism that had taken on a notably Puritan cast.[22] The image of the "Lamp," used by Meyer Abrams to emblematize the expressive aesthetic of the Romantic era, perhaps had an ancestor in the "Inner Light." Certainly the Romantic poets assumed the priesthood of all believers. In fact this side of Romanticism may be viewed as the literary revenge of Dissenting "enthusiasm" for the abuse it had suffered at the hands of the Tory satirists in the preceding century. (The classic-romantic antinomy has this much point at least.) This moralism was passed on to modern literature from a hundred sources: Frank Kermode remarks that even Oscar Wilde's use of the word "immoral" to define art was "not very remote" from the more usual "moral" in the thought of men like Coleridge.[23] The Romantic Image itself always had a decidedly antinomian flavor; the artists insisted on its "uselessness" in order to assert the transcendence by their work of the shallow, petty, well-fed ethical codes of the bourgeois world. Pound could not help inheriting this tendency of the Romantic-Aesthetic movement any more than he could help repeating, in his early days, much high-flown talk about "Beauty." In his case native Americanism brought the Puritan contours within that movement into high relief.

In some later statements Pound professed hatred of Christianity and especially of the Jewish element in it, the "Old

22 From the 1800 Preface to *Lyrical Ballads*.
23 Kermode, *Romantic Image*, 47.

Testy-munk." In part this was merely a repudiation of his youth, when he had apparently had the attitudes of orthodox piety; a church-goer and YMCA member in college, he was moved to write "Ballad of the Goodly Fere" in a state of indignant irritation at the "cheap irreverence" of some young London wits.[24] But more importantly these sentiments reflect the latter-day Gnosticism of the late nineteenth century, which propagated the comfortable delusion that it could hold to the "God of love" of the Gospels while discarding that barbarous vengeful Yahweh of the Old Testament. Anti-Semitism has many sources, this notion being one of the most insidious. Yet even Pound's consequent preference for "Greek deities" had puritanic motives. It was not a repetition of the old Hellenism–Hebraism snobbery, but an outraged reaction to the degeneracy of organized religion: Pound's blasts recall the tirades of Luther at corrupt churchmen. Pound blamed them for a state of things in which "the minute you proclaim that the mysteries exist *at all* you've got to recognize that 95% of yr. contemporaries will not and can not understand one word of what you are driving at." [25] The churches had extinguished the sense of myth as real: for Pound one of the worst in the list of abuses in the Western world that he felt bound to cry out upon.

When we are trying to decide how much weight to give to the Puritan factor in Pound's heritage, it may prove helpful to remember that the tradition of bitter attacks on the abuses of society has not merely an itch to destroy but a tremendous affirmative vision to move it. To build the just city is the aspira-

[24] See "How I Began" (note 3 to Chap. Four); cf. this from "Advice to a Young Poet," *Little Review*, IV (1917), 59: "At twenty I emitted the same kind of asinine generalities regarding Christianity and its beauties that you now let off about poetry." Also cf. *Guide to Kulchur*, 300: "I was brought up in American school and sunday school. Took the stuff for granted, and at one time with great seriousness." The mention of church-going and YMCA membership is in the Yale letters.

[25] *Letters*, 328–29.

tion of all the prophets—one which they dramatize by denouncing the worldly city, and often by going into some form of self-exile. It isn't healthy for a prophet to stay at home. Unfortunately, without willing it the exiled prophet may come perilously close to treason: in this sense the Rome broadcasts carry the voice of the prophet from his mountaintop. If we can disentangle from them Pound's political obsessions and economic panaceas, we may find a substratum of the Hebraic yearning for justice and abhorrence of exploitation. We may even find that, as with some other seers, Pound's blindness to certain facts right under his nose only makes more poignant his farsighted vision of certain truly desirable objectives for Western life and institutions.

The Dangers of an Analogy

I hope this book does not lead anyone to conclude that I believe a discussion of poetics to be equivalent to a discussion of poetry. Nonetheless we must all make some effort to comprehend a poetics, by guesswork or other means, when we propose to read a man's work as anything more than a series of separate poems. Besides, poetics has its own place in the world. Graham Hough and other critics who in the end deplore Pound's influence have already made a case, albeit negatively, for considering the Imagist Revolution "as momentous as the Romantic one of over a century before." [26] In spite of creeping nominalism there are few today who will deny that there was something called Romanticism, or that it had far-reaching effects. What the future will say of modernism, of Imagism's place in it, and of Pound's thought, is more problematical, but none of these are unreal or insubstantial wraiths. In relation to the body of his poetry, it seems enough to conclude that Imagism as discipline

[26] *Image and Experience*, 6.

was the strictest training Pound could have given himself, and there is good evidence that the basic methods involved gave him fresh creative impulses throughout his career. Consistently he sought to concentrate much meaning into a few words, "charging" the words to the utmost degree; he worked at "presentation," seeking the exact proportion between detail and insight; he practiced the art of "living language" in order to capture the "imperfect broken utterances" of natural speech—in fact he employed the latter principle throughout the *Cantos*, colloquializing many languages besides modern English. His art continued to rest on the principle of the "universal in the particular," just as it continued to strive for objective predication, letting realities manifest themselves, rather than settling for subjective affirmation or denial. Many have questioned whether Pound in fact achieved that last goal; such a question cannot be answered here, and I must be content to point to Pound's consistent aim at it. He continued to render the shapes of experience, and to try to enshrine the direct knowledge that differs from our conceptual ones. All the Imagist ingredients stay in his work, in one form or another, although the poetry came to have obvious differences from the Imagist poems of the early period.

The methods that did not change gave to his work a continuing quality of epigrammatic etching. The traditional techniques of the epigram have an affinity with Imagist discipline; to get classic "directness of presentation," Pound said, "one must go back to Catullus, perhaps to the poem which contains *dentes habet*." [27] Actually the epigram is more important in the ancestry of Imagism than the oft-noted *haiku*. Many more of Pound's shorter poems are in the style of the epigram than in that of the *haiku*, and the influence continues through the longer works. Pound departed from classical practice by lessening emphasis on "point" in the old sense, but this was made necessary

[27] *Literary Essays*, 33.

by his decision to render the shapes, the lines of force, of a situation rather than to impose rhetorical structure upon it. With that one proviso, we can see that the incisive statements of the epigram could be well adapted to the presentation of complexes and configurations of experience.

About the *Cantos* there are naturally more complex questions. My concern is simply to assert that the *Cantos* have their roots in Imagist poetics. Between an Imagist poem and a Canto there is a major difference in form, of course, yet the continuity is there too, much like the one that obtains between Impressionism and contemporary art: the *Cantos* are to the short Imagist poems as today's freewheeling sculpture is to the anti-academic picture. In both Imagism and Impressionism we have a breakthrough toward dynamism; and both, by seeking truer representations, ended by breaking the stranglehold of "representationalism." The sense of the isolated "moment," of instantaneity, that inheres in a short Imagist poem had been useful to render shapes of insight or sudden illumination or realization. But Fenollosa taught Pound that the sense of activity is the sense of reality, and large-scale embodiments of it demanded a less constricted form. Moreover, his own *Nekuia*, the sojourn in London, had engendered in him among other things the hope of a "long, endless, leviathanic" poem, an epic "tale of the tribe." [28]

As I have already noted, at about the time when he launched out in earnest on his long poem he defined Imagism in visionary terms that seem especially useful for glossing the first few *Cantos:* "Certain men move in phantasmagoria; the images of their gods, whole countrysides, stretches of hill and forest, travel with them." With Pound traveled the countryside of southern France, northern Italy, and other landscapes that had become part of his mind in various ways; also he was attended by visions of gods, images from the *Metamorphoses*, and many another

[28] See *Letters,* 104 and 294.

locus of "direct knowledge." These are etched into the early *Cantos;* they are what he had to "get down": "The first 11 cantos are preparation of the palette. I *have to* get down all the colours or elements I want for the poem. Some perhaps too enigmatically and abbreviatedly. I hope, heaven help me, to bring them into some sort of design and architecture later." [29] (It is easy to misread that last sentence as implying static conceptions of "form." This he never really desired; his moralist aesthetic forbade such imposed designs. Instead the flow of direct knowledge embodied in the metamorphic tradition is the "figure in the carpet" of the *Cantos.*) [30] In view of this merging of Imagism into reverie and phantasmagoric vision, and in view of the relationship between the precisions of Imagism and the precisions of the *Cantos*, it seems allowable to contend that the *Cantos* are not a repudiation of Imagism but a magnified projection of it.

At this point, however, a great demurrer should be entered. Almost without exception the metaphors that I and others have used to illumine Imagism have been drawn from the visual arts. This is natural enough for a movement that Pound sometimes defined as consisting of a "sort of poetry where painting or sculpture seems as if it were 'just coming over into speech.' " [31] But is there not a danger that these analogies may cause us to overlook the importance of the auditory modality of the *Cantos?* Do not such analogies by their very nature distort our most basic understanding of Pound's art, which is fundamentally that of words spoken? Are we not inviting the misconception that Walter Ong might call "well-wrought-urn-ism"? [32]

[29] *Letters*, 180.
[30] *Letters*, 210.
[31] *Gaudier-Brzeska*, 82.
[32] See Walter J. Ong, "A Dialectic of Aural and Objective Correlatives," first published in *Essays in Criticism*, VIII (1958), reprinted in *Approaches to the Poem: Modern Essays in the Analysis and Interpretation of Poetry*, ed. John Oliver Perry (San Francisco, 1965).

From very different viewpoints, Charles Olson and others have warned us that we neglect the oral and aural character of poetry at our peril. Ong also makes a good case against the "tactile and visualist bias" of twentieth-century criticism. Obviously, if we take these visual-arts analogies too literally, we shall think of poems as things closed, fixed, impersonal, and perhaps lifeless. We shall pay too much attention to irrelevant kinds of external form, and, if the New Criticism is any example, we may find ourselves in a self-enclosing, ever-constricting critical world of conceits, tropes, finer and finer ironies. These are bad enough, but the visualist pitfall has even worse effects: since it is an ontological misconception, it prevents us from knowing the real being of a poem. Very likely it will involve us in personalist and subjectivist dilemmas: as Ong points out, the whole "subjective-objective classification" is "derivative from an unreflective visualist notion of reality." [33] Marshall McLuhan makes the same point by quoting Gilbert Ryle, to the effect that the visualist model of the process of perception somehow makes us seem like prisoners in a cell, fairly sure of something within but most uncertain as to what is going on outside.[34] Since we are all heartily sick of the unhappy splitting-up of the world into *res extensa* and *res cogitans*, such charges are a telling indictment. An aural idea of perception, on the other hand, involves us as integral parts of our world. A world of sound is "loaded with direct personal significance for the hearer," and to respond to it we must open ourselves up, come out of subjective prisons.[35] In short there are a hundred good general and specific

[33] Ong, in *Approaches to the Poem*, 252.
[34] Marshall McLuhan, *The Gutenberg Galaxy: The Making of Typographic Man* (Toronto, 1962), 72–73. Ong, McLuhan, and Hugh Kenner (see note 45 to Chap. Five) are on an anti-visualist crusade as part of their vigorous Catholic assertions of the reality of the objective world.
[35] McLuhan, quoting J. C. Carothers, 19. Not the least of the dangers of the visual-arts analogies is the "representationalist" inertia that still inheres in them even after the revolutions in modern art.

reasons to beware of relying on visual analogies to conceive of poetic processes.

In my discussion of Pound's poetics I have been at some pains to subordinate the visual, since I had discovered when I began the study that neither Imagist theory nor its practice were predominantly visualist. Looking merely at the connotations of the name has deceived many critics; the "Image" presents "complexes," not visual scenes or models. Far more important to Pound's Imagism than any *ut pictura poesis* theory was the great discovery of the principle of "living language," that oral basis of man's behavior. Like other poetries, Imagism made some use of visual detail; more than most poetries, it sought a clarity that may be usefully emblematized by visual or tactile metaphors. In an Imagist poem Pound is trying to make us "see" or "grasp" something. But he always eschewed pictorialism, and never subscribed to such demands as Hulme's for constant visualization. On the awareness of these differentiations hangs an adequate understanding of Imagism. Once they are grasped, however, the comparisons to visual arts have an undeniable usefulness.

The question then becomes, does Pound's poetry change sufficiently after the Imagist period to require us to abandon the visual-arts analogies entirely? Must we drop after a certain point such terms as "sculptural," "etching," and the rest? Evidently we could look at changes in Pound's approach like the use of *logopoeia* as a breaking out of visualist constrictions—but only if we overvalue the visual element in Imagism. Therefore I treat the categories of *melopoeia* and *phanopoeia* not so much as totally new and unheralded modes, but as mostly rearrangements in the interest of clear distinctions. The three categories are nicely separable, whereas Imagism had always been more of a mixed bag than its name implied. After all, Pound had been employing some of the tactics of *logopoeia* and *melopoeia* all along.

There are new emphases on these two modes, of course. At about the same time that he began to use *logopoeia* with enthusiasm, he wrote to Margaret Anderson (in the same letter where he stated his desire "to go on with my long poem" and "to hear the music of a lost dynasty") that "I desire also to resurrect the art of the lyric, I mean words to be sung." [36] In other words he began to formalize his interest in *melopoeia*. But nobody could maintain that this was a new discovery for him.

The clue is in the ease with which he moved from interest to interest. There is no repudiation of earlier aesthetics, such as Imagism itself had required in 1912. He proceeded naturally through this dramatic heightening and redefining of categories, without laments about having been stuck in one place. So the changes that do occur in the poetry, it seems to me, are mostly those involved in changing from short forms to longer ones. To the extent that the continuous sequence of poems demanded a different vocal basis, and to the extent that he emulated the epic or oral tradition, these changes involve a more oral-aural mode and response. But Imagistic precision was not given up: the poem still consisted of Luminous Details, and the technique for those was "presentation." There was still that etched quality to his work.

I would cheerfully admit that the visual-arts terminology sometimes obscures that very sense of activity and force that is so vital to his art. It can lead to neglect of the movement of his line, which always seems to have a powerful drive behind it even when the verse is stately and calm. The subtle music of the lines has often been celebrated, better by other poets than by critics or historians of ideas, and there is a whole field of possibilities for commentary on their surge, on the movement of voice rising, pausing, picking up, catching the phrase and moving with it. In the apparently artless business of moving from

[36] *Letters,* 128.

word to word Pound may turn out to be one of the most artful poets in the language. But once again it was the precision of effect that Imagism demanded that prepared him to deal so exactly with this matter, as it was the principle of "living language" that taught him the importance and potentiality of cadence in the first place. The practiced ear that brought forth all the dynamism in a line from the *Cantos* was trained on the delicacies of a poem like "In a Station of the Metró," or "The Garden."

Therefore, while we must be aware of limitations to our visual-arts analogies, I see no profit in running to the other extreme of using equally restrictive aural metaphors. Pound's work is not what a true oral poet would construct. He is no blind Homer—nor even a "partially sighted" Joyce, giving us as the masterpiece of his career an oral history of mankind. (Pound's response to a sample of *Finnegans Wake* is instructive: "Up to the present I make nothing of it whatever. Nothing so far as I make out, nothing short of divine vision or a new cure for the clapp can possibly be worth all the circumambient peripherization." [37] No doubt it is too much to expect one great experimentalist genius to appreciate the more extreme work of another, but if Pound's own interests had been exclusively oral we might have expected more sympathy for Joyce's telescoping of the layers of spoken language.) Pound is rather a highly eclectic poet, intensely aware of what oral values are and what they can do for his work, but with his eyes wide open. Being a man of the Gutenburgian age, he knows enough not to be tempted to chase the ghost of noble savagery that flits through the more primitivist pronouncements that our age must recover its oral basis. For Pound, the knowledge that is "in the air" can be passed through texts, as well as by word of mouth. It seems to have been part of his aim to prove that language does not have to

[37] *Letters,* 202.

be deadened to be written down, that the poet's voice can be preserved in print. As Charles Olson points out, the poets who made "the revolution of the ear, 1910" are those who have taken most advantage of "typographical rhetoric." [38] They do not ignore the potentialities of type and print, but exploit them. Like any important poem, the *Cantos* profits by being read aloud; but the reading can be done with all the more skill because of the formal arrangements on the page.

Form was one of the values to which Pound was utterly committed. Not a form of objects—not "well-wrought-urn-ism"—but a form of events, of process, of lines of force as Fenollosa apprehended them: "Transferences of power." Sight alone can never come to the conception of a universe so full of vital energies that forces are being transferred constantly, but without sight we would have only a vague roaring in our ears from such apprehension. Form, for Pound, is an attempt to focus on the loci of these transferences. His is dynamic form, to be sure. As he once put it: "Forma to the great minds of at least one epoch meant something more than dead pattern or fixed opinion. 'The light of the DOER, as it were a form cleaving to it' meant an ACTIVE pattern, a pattern that set things in motion." [39] Reading a line from a Canto, we must have a sense that something is "going on" all the time; the words do not simply lie in limp patterns, the poem is something happening rather than something over with. But it also has a fixedness, a dance, even in its movement: Pound was a Vorticist, a man who believes that powerful force creates and maintains form. The vortex is a figure for the reconciliation of those mighty opposites, dynamic and static, in a shape whose fixedness is dependent on a certain intensity of movement.

Two passages from Pound's commentaries on the most ener-

[38] Olson, "Projective Verse," 393–94.
[39] *Polite Essays*, 51.

getic of his fellow Vorticists are of special interest here. The first is from a review of Wyndham Lewis' novel *Tarr:*

"Tarr" really gets at something in his last long discussion with Anastasya, when he says that art "has no inside." This is a condition of art, "*to have no* inside, nothing you cannot see. It is not something impelled like a machine by a little egoistic inside."

"Deadness, in the limited sense in which we use that word, is the first condition of art. The second is absence of *soul*, in the sentimental human sense. The lines and masses of a statue are its soul."

Joyce says something of the sort very differently, he is full of technical scholastic terms: "*stasis, kinesis,*" etc.[40]

Actually Joyce, or rather Stephen Dedalus, had used these terms in a moral sense; he wanted art to avoid exciting either desire or loathing. Pound's rumination with them seems to indicate that he, on the other hand, was thinking mostly about the question of form in art. This indication is substantiated by the second passage, which concerns Gaudier–Brzeska's statue of Pound himself:

The bust of me was most striking, perhaps, two weeks before it was finished. I do not mean to say that it was better, it was perhaps a *kinesis*, whereas it is now a *stasis;* but before the back was cut out, and before the middle lock was cut down, there was in the marble a titanic energy, it was like a great stubby catapult, the two masses bent for a blow. I do not mean that he was wrong to go on with it. Great art is perhaps a stasis. The unfinished stone caught the eye. Maybe it would have wearied it. . . .

There is in the final condition of the stone a great calm.[41]

Clearly Pound is ambivalent; he is attracted by *kinesis*, that in-

---

[40] *Literary Essays*, 430. Pound's quotations are inexact, but it doesn't matter here.

[41] *Gaudier-Brzeska*, 49.

dispensable component of a sense of reality, but his aesthetic demands that *stasis* be valued also. The reasons why his aesthetic made such a demand are entangled in the history of the Romantic Image tradition, and in a revulsion against vitalism. Briefly, some artists got fed up with fatuous presentations of warm, sanguine, comradely values in the name of "life." Hence Yeats desires to write a poem "cold and passionate as the dawn"; hence Lewis makes his statement about deadness in art, or proclaims in *Blast* that " 'Life' is a hospital for the weak and incompetent." [42] As Richard Ellmann notes, "the religion of life keeps most of its Edwardian adherents, but it has begun to stir up its own atheists and agnostics." [43] Assertions of death begin to counterbalance those of life; Freud arrives at the idea of the death instinct, reported in *Beyond the Pleasure Principle*, as a result of what happened in 1914. The cult of health begins to seem less interesting than the diseased values of *poètes maudits*, and the antinomian urge enters to reinforce assertions of death and stasis against the Rotarian values of life and growth. There had always been a striving within the Romantic Image tradition for stillness-in-motion images of various kinds: back of these there were Coleridge's "reconciliation of opposite or discordant qualities," Nietzsche's Apollonian-and-Dionysian, and the great philosophic traditions of fixity in flux, permanence in change, the one in the many, and behind these the great Judaeo-Christian paradox of a god both immanent and transcendent, inhabiting a realm of permanence and yet actively present in his transient creation. So Pound's Vorticist idea of force and form was in a

[42] "Vorteces and Notes by Wyndham Lewis," *Blast* No. 1 (June 20, 1914), 130. Behind such statements was the influence of a German aesthetician, Wilhelm Worringer.

[43] Richard Ellmann, "Two Faces of Edward," in *Edwardians and Late Victorians*, English Institute Essays, 1959 (New York, 1960), 210.

sense entirely traditional, and his ambivalence about *kinesis* and *stasis* was predictable.

The remarkable thing is that in the poetry of the *Cantos* he seems actually to have attained this paradoxical ideal. Today Pound's admirers respond, I suspect, far more readily to the *kinesis* in his poetry; the quarrel with vitalism has faded, and the urgency of the values of *stasis* has consequently diminished. The struggles of the Yeats-Pound-Eliot generation to maintain the paradox of force and form in their controlling images—for Yeats pre-eminently the dancer, for Pound the vortex, for Eliot the still point of the turning world—have seemed too costly or too compromising for contemporary art, which is more interested in resolving the paradox on the side of force, movement, kinetic flux. Our arts now embrace a kind of vitalism the older modernists rejected; this is consonant with the new obsessive striving for immediacy. True, these new arts are following trends begun by Pound among others: they seek a mythic communion of "direct knowledge" rather than conceptual communication; their dream is a participatory "tale of the tribe" rather than an interpretability suitable for abstract commentary. They have wholly adopted Fenollosa's thesis that action is reality, and realigned themselves toward oral, dramatic fulfillment. But in their drive to power they have forgotten a rage for order: in their headlong plunge into the Dionysian flux of immanent mystic unity they have abandoned the hold that Pound and the rest kept on the Apollonian values of individuation, transcendence, and permanence. With their programmatic formlessness and scorn for ego-understanding, our arts make real some of the dreams, but also some of the nightmares, of the earlier generation. Yeats came to fear that Pound had initiated a slide into chaos foretold when Pater insisted on experience rather than the fruit of experience: "Did Pater foreshadow a poetry, a philosophy, where the individual is nothing, the flux of the *Cantos* of Ezra Pound, objects without contour as in *Le Chef d'oeuvre inconnu*, human experience no longer shut into brief lives . . . ?" [44] There is no doubt a sense in which Yeats's question must be answered in the affirmative, and many of to-day's artists proudly claim the heritage of the "flux of the *Cantos*." Nevertheless, to understand Pound in his own terms we must go back to the basic paradox, to form as well as force, to the *stasis* of the visual-arts analogies as well as the *kinesis* of oral dynamism.

What reveals itself throughout the whole spectrum of his work is a kind of registering energy. When he likened the Troubadours' sexual awareness to a wireless telegraph mechanism he surely had in mind his own ability for "registering movements in the invisible aether," his openness to forces of all kinds. He seems to have cultivated this registering mechanism, and in a sense might have found it appropriately described by Yvor Winters' malicious phrase about him, "a sensibility without a mind." Certainly he had little use for what Winters meant by

[44] Kermode in *Romantic Image* quotes this significant passage on p. 63. Kermode neglects Nietzsche's influence, but although I can find no conclusive evidence I feel sure that the Apollo-Dionysus antinomy was in the background of this aspect of modernism. Nietzsche's theory was that Greek tragedy was engendered from the intercourse or synthesizing of the forces represented by these deities: this conception is in fact an emblem of unions of force and form, universal and particular, even aural and visual. For Nietzsche, Dionysus is characterized by life-force, mystic union or oneness, and "the spirit of music"; Apollo by plastic or shaping powers, individuation and selfhood, and the visual modalities of plastic arts and dreams. Hence Pound's union of aural and visual, or kinetic and static, is a summation of this tendency. Actually the antinomy has almost endless suggestiveness: typology was similarly structured, since it combined history (which has form and is thus Apollonian) with Eternal Recurrence (Dionysian). And it hardly needs saying that the Dionysian idea prefigures many kinds of contemporary primitivisms (including the political ones to which so many modernists were attracted) and emphases on myth, powers of the liberated unconscious, etc. However, I am much indebted to the rest of Kermode's analysis, and especially to his brilliant summation of the characteristics of the Romantic Image on p. 44, which ends by finding it "fixed yet constantly moving."

"mind." " 'Thought' as Browning understood it—'ideas' as the term is current, are poor two-dimensional stuff, a scant, scratch covering. 'Damn ideas, anyhow.' An idea is only an imperfect induction from fact." [45] Such a statement is typically modernist, and traditional in important ways too; but what did Pound himself feel took the place of such "thought"? Obviously, a vaster world of direct knowledge, available to be registered by the sensibilities of those who understand the interpretative function of the arts in a vital universe. If he is surely a "poet of reality," he is just as surely determined to extend the boundaries of what we call real. Charles Olson scoffs at poetry "never off the dead-spot of description. . . . referential to reality. And that a p. poor crawling actuarial 'real'—good enough to keep banks and insurance companies, plus mediocre governments etc. But not Poetry's *Truth* like my friends from the American Underground cry and spit in the face of 'Time.' " [46] The greatest figures in the literary tradition of the Western world have always been concerned to assert the "higher truth" of poetry, and Pound is one of their most convinced and passionate inheritors.

In the end Pound's "poetry of reality" depends on his boundless faith in language. He truly believed that words did not merely describe or point to real things, but could really body them forth. Far from wishing that poetry could be made with something other than words, with objects or with bodily sensations, he believed instead that words could get closer to the inner nature of reality than other apprehensions of experience. This is not to say that he believed that "words alone are certain good," or valued *verba* over *res:* on the contrary, he felt that the highest function of language could be achieved only by a severe restriction on verbalism, a discipline that would remove the "curse of mediacy" from words by making language totally ef-

[45] *Literary Essays,* 267.
[46] "Letter to Elaine Feinstein," in *The New American Poetry: 1945–1960,* ed. Donald M. Allen (New York, 1960), 399.

ficient, making every word count. The way to free language from that curse, from that condition in which "it is bound to obscure what it seeks to reveal," was a registration of reality which would so absorb the words that no inexactness would be left to get between thing and reader.[47] Seeking this registering by "presentation," by making the words "strike the senses as nearly as possible" as experience itself would, and by charging the words with that vitality and force that Fenollosa commended, the artist could achieve an "Image": not a copy, but a revealing presentation of a thing that essentialized it, showed its substance, manifested the lines of force of its morphological shape. In this sense, the Image is not just "indistinguishable from the thing": it is more striking, more lasting, than any given perception of the thing. What Pound saw in Egyptian statuary is what he wanted: an art of incarnation. To be sure, it is the reverse of an orthodox incarnation: it is flesh made word. One can feel sure that Pound responded to the message Joyce embedded in the "Oxen of the Sun" chapter of *Ulysses:* "Mark me now. In woman's womb word is made flesh but in the spirit of the maker all flesh that passes becomes the word that shall not pass away." [48] These conceptions depend on an idea of language in which the word has, through the centuries, in the "magic moment" received reality into it. In this moment, all analogies for language are transcended.

---

[47] These last two phrases are from Cassirer's *Language and Myth,* 7. Like St. Augustine, Pound wanted us *in verbis verum amare, non verba* ("to love the truth in words, not the words").

[48] James Joyce, *Ulysses,* Modern Library ed. (New York, 1934), 385.

INDEX

INDEX OF POUND TITLES

(Included are books, poems, and the most relevant essays. No distinction has been made here between page and footnote references. Essays marked with asterisks were part of a series in the *New Age* [1911–12] called "I Gather the Limbs of Osiris.")

SUBJECT INDEX